Going Home
without
Going Crazy

How to Get Along with Your Parents & Family (Even When They Push Your Buttons)

ANDRA MEDEA

HILLSBORO PUBLIC LIBRARIES
Hillsboro, OR
Member of Washington County
COOPERATIVE LIBRARY SERVICES

New Harbinger Publications, Inc.

Publisher's Note

This publication is designed to provide accurate and authoritative information in regard to the subject matter covered. It is sold with the understanding that the publisher is not engaged in rendering psychological, financial, legal, or other professional services. If expert assistance or counseling is needed, the services of a competent professional should be sought.

Distributed in Canada by Raincoast Books

Copyright © 2006 by Andra Medea
New Harbinger Publications, Inc.
5674 Shattuck Avenue
Oakland, CA 94609

Cover design by Amy Shoup; Acquired by Melissa Kirk;
Text design by Tracy Marie Carlson; Edited by Kayla Sussell

All Rights Reserved
Printed in the United States of America

Library of Congress Cataloging-in-Publication Data

Medea, Andra.
  Going home without going crazy : how to get along with your parents and family (even when they push your buttons) / Andra Medea. — 1st printing.
    p. cm.
  ISBN-13: 978-1-57224-449-8
  ISBN-10: 1-57224-449-6 4055 9030 7/09
  1. Family—Psychological aspects. 2. Interpersonal conflict. 3. Conflict management. I. Title.
  HQ734.M4485 2006
  646.7'8—dc22

                                                            2006017702

New Harbinger Publications' Web site address: www.newharbinger.com

08   07   06

10   9   8   7   6   5   4   3   2   1

First printing

This book is dedicated to my mother, Emily Thomas, who would have thoroughly enjoyed this.

Contents

Acknowledgments

As with any book, there are more people who deserve thanks than can be listed in one place. This then, is a partial list of the good-hearted individuals and fine minds who contributed to this project.

First I have to thank Bonny Flaster, who has made all these conflict projects possible by her tenacious belief and determined goodwill.

I also need to thank the many students from my classes at Northwestern, DePaul, and the University of Chicago, whose hard work and resourcefulness contributed to this project.

Further contributors include:

Penny Pope, who has repeatedly demonstrated diplomacy above and beyond the call of valor.

Kathleen Thompson and Mike Nowak, for their ongoing support and willingness to experiment.

The Rev. Wes Thompson, who consistently came up with excellent advice when family members were at their wits' end.

Zak Mucha, for a wonderful sense of humor in infuriating situations.

Carla Thomas, for her excellent advice on handling small, fractious children.

Riva Lehrer, for introducing me to one ingenious soul after another.

Penny Wilson, for her inspired examples of indirect language.

My good friend V., who has been immensely helpful at every turn.

Melissa Kirk, acquisitions editor at New Harbinger, who started this project and shepherded it through its many stages, and Heather Mitchener, editorial director, who helped the final book take shape.

And finally, Kayla Sussell, the remarkably patient editor who wrestled every last comma and paragraph into place.

Introduction

It's not always easy dealing with your family of origin. You may look forward to visiting them or you may be filled with dread. Even the best of families sometimes fight.

Families may fight silently, with no more noise than the ominous clatter of dishes being cleared away, or so furiously that all the neighbors hear every word. Yet conflict itself isn't the problem. Families grow, change, and re-create themselves. Inevitably, this can cause conflict. The problem isn't that families fight, but *how* they fight. Sane, healthy conflict solves problems and allows everyone to move on with dignity. Unhealthy fighting leaves problems unresolved as family members descend into sniping, bickering, or outright abuse.

You may have had quite enough of your family's brand of fighting, and be looking for a better way. If so, this book is for you. The purpose of this book is to show you the hidden patterns in every conflict, so you can find more effective ways to deal with your family and break out of unhealthy patterns.

My approach to solving these problems is based on my model of the Conflict Continuum. This hands-on approach was refined over the years that I taught conflict management at Northwestern University, DePaul, and the University of Chicago. Most of my students were adults with commitments at home, work, and with their families. They were there because the usual suggestions for solving conflicts simply had not worked for them.

I didn't psychoanalyze my students or ask them to psychoanalyze themselves; I only wanted them to be able to solve their problems. This new approach worked for them and, hopefully, it will work for you too.

My first book that presented this new approach was called *Conflict Unraveled: Fixing Problems at Work and in Families*. Melissa Kirk, acquisitions editor at New Harbinger, read it and asked if I would do something similar for people dealing with their family of origin. This book is the result. It is more hands-on, more interactive, and more focused on that small group of blood relations who are best equipped to drive you crazy.

The focus of this approach is behavior. This means I won't ask you to delve into your past very much. Instead, the primary focus will be on what you can do *now* to solve conflicts that are happening *now*. There isn't much you can do to change the past. But you can do quite a bit to change what happens now and when you visit your folks next week.

In accord with the emphasis on practicality, this book also focuses on the ways you manage your actions. You are the master of your actions. When you make a plan that depends on your actions, the odds are in your favor. Other family members are outside your control, and thus they give you less promising odds. To keep the odds in your favor, stick with matters you control.

HOW TO USE THIS BOOK

This book is designed to show you how to recognize conflicts, and then it offers choices for how you might solve those conflicts. It is divided into roughly three parts.

The first section (chapter 1) deals with the basics: your brain under stress. Humans come with hardwiring flaws, and your brain will malfunction under too much pressure. It's important for you to know these pitfalls, understand how to keep your head clear despite strain, and know what to do when other brains are malfunctioning all around you. All other skills depend on you having a functioning brain, so this is the place to start.

The second section (chapters 2 through 5) is about recognizing the different types of conflict. My model shows how different types of conflict operate by different rules and respond to different techniques. This section will explain some seemingly inexplicable behavior from your family. Better yet, these chapters point to specific solutions. Just as you would want the right medicine to treat the right disorder, these chapters will help you make sense of conflict and see what's needed to solve it.

The third and final section (chapters 6 through 9) has material on solving common breakdowns. For example, to stay clear of common trip wires, check chapter 6 on triggering family conflict. To avoid the communication breakdowns that plague many families, check chapter 7 on direct and indirect language. These are everyday, practical skills that can save you a world of trouble.

This book is designed to be used interactively, posing questions to you, for you, and about you. It's meant to be worked with, not just thought about. For working with the exercises, keep a separate notebook or journal. This separate notebook is essential so that you can write down your thoughts and answers to the questions posed in the exercises. But to get the maximum benefit, it's best to write down your ideas while you read. You know how it is—you'll have a great idea or insight and neglect to write it down, and the next day you find that you can't recall exactly what it was. Capture those great thoughts by writing them down.

You may be having a tough time with your family. They may never change, but you can; you can permanently shift your behavior so that their problems don't have the same effect on you. Conflict may be exhausting, but it's also liberating once you learn to break out of your old patterns.

Good luck on your journey. You may even enjoy it.

Note that all names and identifying information have been changed to protect the guilty and innocent alike. Some stories have been combined for the sake of brevity.

Chapter One

Overdosing on Adrenaline

The phone rings. It's your mom.

She says three words and immediately you feel trapped, beset, and somehow wrong. Whatever you say is wrong. Mom asks about your job. You start to answer, perhaps speaking quickly, because you know that if you leave a gap, your mom will offer you advice. You're not fast enough; she offers her advice. You try to change the subject. She offers you advice about changing the subject.

Maneuvering for a more neutral topic, you bring up your sister's upcoming wedding. Quickly you realize this is a mistake. There's a pregnant pause, as your mother, too, realizes you're both on thin ice. You know she wants to tell you what the neighbors are saying. She knows she wants to tell you, and she also knows that you will not be happy to hear it. You both hold your breath. She takes the plunge.

You notice, by now, that a throbbing headache has started up behind one ear and is working its way behind your eyes. The force of your headache is pushing on your brain case.

Ten minutes into this short conversation your mouth is dry and it feels as though the top of your head will explode. You eye the window wondering if you can put down the phone and quietly make a break for it without her noticing. Mom asks why you haven't come to visit. You sit there openmouthed, your mind a total blank. You can think of absolutely nothing to say.

Then your dad gets on the line. He wants to know why you've upset your mother.

You could swear this was the work of a secret parent cabal who get together to manipulate the market on migraine medication and antidepressants. (Meanwhile, in an alternate universe, moms gather together over coffee to talk about their kids. They'd like to know what's wrong.)

Everyone has a family of origin and almost no one knows how to cope with them. You love them; they drive you crazy. You wish holidays and phone calls didn't always end up like your own private reality show where you never get to change the channel.

This can all be changed, without you having to move to Nepal or swear to never see your family again. And it all starts with flooding.

FLOODING

Flooding occurs when an adrenaline overload overwhelms parts of the brain. Have you ever been so upset you can't think, can't speak, can barely cope? That's flooding. Landmark research on flooding was done by Dr. John Gottman. In their 1995 book Gottman, Silver, and other researchers worked with lab equipment that recorded and monitored changes in the body and brain when people were stressed. Gottman, a specialist in couple conflict, had many intriguing insights that can be found in his book *Why Marriages Succeed or Fail*. You may already know something about flooding from the fight-or-flight syndrome, where the more primitive parts of the brain override the more advanced parts. The result is knee-jerk fear or aggression and a distinct lack of levelheaded reason. However, with Gottman's work we can now add many important and useful insights.

You can expect flooding to affect you both physically and mentally. We'll start by looking at the physical symptoms, because they provide important clues that your brain is starting to malfunction. These physical symptoms act like an early warning system. The physical signs are also easier to spot. Then we'll look at ways you can clear your head and get control of yourself again.

Your ultimate goal is to control flooding rather than allow it to control you.

Physical Signs of Flooding

In many people, the first sign of flooding is a tightness or pounding in the head. That's your blood pressure rising. The throbbing headache that you associate with your parents or your Aunt Pauline is not just the result of your family's dynamics; it is also a physical sign you've begun flooding.

Your heart may start pounding or crashing against your chest. Your breathing may become shallow, leaving you short of breath. Your face may get flushed. Fair-skinned people turn red, while dark-skinned people get darker. You may get sweaty palms or a dry "cotton" mouth. Some people report tingling in their fingers and toes.

You may also experience a lack of coordination. Stressed, you may fumble for a pen, or not be able to get your keys in the door. You may drop things. Small, everyday motions become difficult.

It's important that you learn to recognize your own physical symptoms when flooding hits. This is your first warning that you're not operating at your best. As stated above, the physical symptoms are usually the easiest to spot. You may never notice that you've stopped thinking clearly, but you can notice when it feels as if the top of your head may lift off.

Here is a checklist of the physical symptoms of flooding. Check off those that are familiar to you, or write them down in your separate notebook.

Physical Symptoms Checklist

☐ Throbbing head

☐ Shallow breathing

☐ Flushed face

☐ Pounding heart

☐ Dry mouth

☐   Sweating palms

☐   Fumbling small motions (can't get keys in door)

These symptoms are your early warning system against flooding. Once you know you're at risk for flooding, you can change what happens.

CONTROLLING THE PHYSICAL SIGNS OF FLOODING

An adrenaline overload is largely a physical reaction that can be controlled with physical solutions. You can snap out of flooding by engaging in large muscle actions.

For example, you might go for a walk outside or close the door and do some quick sit-ups. If you're talking on the phone with a maddening relative, you could swing your arms vigorously or do deep knee bends. If you're in a situation where you can't suddenly break into calisthenics, do *isometrics*. These are muscle-building exercises in which you contract and release muscles in small movements that are barely visible. For example, you might press your arms against your chair or press your palms against a wall or door.

Deep breathing also helps. Flooding is apt to cause your breathing to become shallow, so reverse that. Breathe deeply. Whether you're in the privacy of your room or in the spotlight giving your sister's wedding toast, you can always control your breath.

HEADING OFF FLOODING IN KIDS

Singing and laughing will also turn back flooding. They are particularly good in preventing flooding when dealing with kids. Let's say you've packed the kids in the car and have headed off to your folks. It's now five hours later, everyone's tired and cranky, and a fight has broken out in the backseat. Your head is pounding and you're about to start screaming at them. Clearly, you're flooding.

Instead of yelling at the kids, try singing at them at the top of your lungs. Or, when the kids turn irritable, get *them* to start singing. Singing encourages deep breathing and lowers adrenaline levels. It's also easier on everyone's nerves.

Singing when you're angry is so absurd that it gets people laughing, which is also great for heading off flooding. After all, if you're stressed about seeing your parents, your kids will pick up on your tension and start flooding, too. Then, they might start acting out around your parents—just when you need it the least.

Amy Dickinson, the advice columnist, offers this great tip for getting kids to settle down and stop fighting with each other. When they start whining and complaining, have them sing their complaints about each other. When they complain about being at Grandpa's away from their videos, have them sing that, too. They can sing only so long before bursting into laughter; that will clear flooding not only in the kids but in nearby grown-ups, as well.

POINTERS FOR NEUTRALIZING FLOODING

Here's a list of physical actions that can counteract flooding and help you clear your head:

- Making large muscle actions, like walking, swinging your arms, or lifting large objects

- Doing isometrics, like reaching down and trying to lift your own chair while you're sitting in it

- Breathing slow, deep breaths

- Getting some more space, going outside

- Relaxing your muscles

- Unclenching your fists

- Singing

- Laughing

HEADING OFF FLOODING IN SOMEONE ELSE

These same techniques apply if you should need to get someone else to stop flooding. For instance, you can get that person to do something physical. You might tell your sister, "Mary, I want to hear you out on this, but I need to get something upstairs. Could we walk while we talk about this?" Then take Mary up several flights of stairs. Mary will become calmer and more cooperative at the top of the stairs than she would have been at the bottom.

If your brother is flooding, try handing him a large, heavy box. A woman I know once pulled a man out of a full inarticulate rant by handing him a large box of books. His muscles had to work to hold the books, his head cleared, and he stopped shouting. The phenomenon is that physical. This is a clear illustration of exactly how physical the phenomenon can be.

Now you know the basics of flood control: that is, how to recognize the physical symptoms and how to pull out of the flooding reaction. Now let's take a look at the mental and emotional factors that come into play.

Mental Signs of Flooding

Flooding essentially "shorts out" the higher parts of the brain. Among other things, this results in trouble with

- Logic

- Language

- Problem-solving

For instance, once you start flooding, you may suddenly be unable to get any words out. You may start talking as if you're brain-impaired: "Mom! You told— ? Wh— But— How could you!!"

At that point, it's evident that flooding has affected your brain's language centers. You suddenly go from being a reasonably intelligent, articulate person to feeling like a tongue-tied fool. But the problem isn't you—it's the flooding.

Any kind of logical thinking may have problems under flooding. For example, suppose your father fires a question at you about your plans for the future. Suddenly your mind becomes a complete blank and you can think of nothing to say. You feel like an idiot.

In fact, you do have plans for your future—you think about it all the time. The problem is when you are suddenly put on the spot, you flood and your mind goes blank. Even worse, flooding it can turn you into a sitting duck if other members of your family decide to add to your embarrassment by firing questions at you that you are suddenly unable to answer.

Instead of getting flustered, take a moment to breathe. Press your elbows against the arms of your chair to help clear your head. Then answer their questions, if you like.

Additional breakdowns in your thinking include the following:

- Circular or jumbled thinking

- An inability to absorb information

- An inability to find options

We'll look at each of these in turn.

CIRCULAR OR JUMBLED THINKING

Flooding disrupts your ability to think in organized ways. Jumbled, disjointed thoughts may start spinning through your head, moving too fast to follow. Your thoughts may run in circles: "I'll never be good enough, they'll only make fun of me. Dad will get that look on his face and it just goes to show that I'll never be good enough. . . ."

This scrambled, circular thinking can make it impossible to hold your own in a conversation. You feel helpless. You can't put together a simple explanation or an ordinary thought. As stated previously, this would be a good time to breathe deeply or do isometrics. For instance, you might put your hands under the table and push yourself straight up, as if you were trying to lift the table. Once you feel your mind clear, you'll be in a better position to answer coherently.

Someone else who's flooding may also exhibit jumbled, circular thinking. For instance, suppose your sister's upset and you ask her what's wrong. Her words tumble out in a rambling muddle that goes on until your head hurts. After ten minutes, you still don't know what the problem is and you're sorry you asked.

The jumble occurs partly because your sister has lost the ability to do sequence. She can't think clearly. Her mind has muddled together unrelated wrongs and slights, so you can't make sense of any of it. It's a mess even to her, and she's likely to flood even more out of sheer frustration.

One way to help your sister pull out of flooding is to ask her sequence questions. For example, when she pauses for air, ask her what happened first. Once that part's clear, ask her what happened next. You'll see her struggle to clarify her thoughts, and she'll begin talking more slowly and coherently. These are positive signs that her head is clearing and she's coming down from flooding.

FLOODING IS CONTAGIOUS

If someone is flooding and obviously upset, a natural response is to try to get him to calm down. However, there's a catch to this: flooding is contagious. This means that even while your sister is venting and testing your patience, you are flooding and losing your ability to follow her.

When someone around you is flooding, you must attend to your own flooding first. It's like the safety directions on the air mask in an airplane: first put on your own mask and then attend to anyone else. You can't help anyone if your brain isn't functioning. Once you have that in hand, then you can see to the other person.

INABILITY TO TAKE IN INFORMATION

Another mental symptom of flooding is that people lose their ability to listen to facts. You've seen this often enough: "Once he gets mad, there's no getting through. I may as well be talking to the wall."

These people aren't ignoring you; it's actually a physical problem that stems from flooding. They've lost the ability to take in new information. You could agree, disagree, talk about the weather—it would make no difference. They can't hear you. You may have had the unsettling experience of having someone continue yelling at you after you've agreed with her. She's not trying to drive you crazy; she never heard you in the first place.

This is a time to bring out some flood control techniques. Ask her to take a walk with you or ask her what happened first. Keep your voice low and calm, and wait until her voice loses its overwrought edge. Then say what you wanted to say. By then, she might be able to hear you.

Of course, the same breakdown can happen to you. For instance, you might grow upset while talking on the phone, and come back to the conversation only to realize you have no idea what the other person said in the last several minutes. Don't jump into the argument; it's time to breathe and move around. There's certainly no point in getting into an argument when you have no idea what has been going on.

LOSS OF OPTIONS

Another mental hazard of flooding is that your options disappear. Whatever's going on, you feel as if you have no choice. At that moment, you may feel that you have to do something, yet the only thing you can think of is extremely unwise: for example, storm away from the dinner table, tell off Uncle Ray, punch your brother.

The reality may be that you have several dozen other options, but that may become clear only later, after you've made a mess of things. When you feel as though you simply have no choice, opt to take a break instead. Go outside, go for a walk. Simply disconnect from things for a while. Once your brain starts working again, more options will present themselves to you.

SUGGESTIBILITY

Another common problem is that people become highly suggestible while flooding. Say you're having a difficult visit with your mother after her recent divorce. She bursts out with, "Why don't you just go back to your father!" Flooding, you grab your coat and leave for your father's.

That would be fine if you wanted to see your father but, in fact, you may have been at your mother's house because you've had quite enough of the man. You wanted to see her, and the last thing you need is to be batted between the two of them like a cat toy. Nonetheless, if she suggests this awful idea to you while you're flooding, you're entirely likely to do it, just because you're flooding.

Before you do anything impulsive, check your physical symptoms. Is your head throbbing? Is your breathing ragged? Are you short of breath? If so, just stop, breathe, and perhaps talk a walk. Decide what to do after you calm down.

URGENCY

Another problem with flooding is that often you feel that you must act *now!* You must storm out of the house, find the perfect comeback, show them you can't be talked to that way, and do it this very instant.

Actually, short of a fire in the sofa, there's very little you must do now. The family argument that has driven you to the edge has been going on since you were twelve. There's really nothing urgent about it. Your mother may have ordered you back to your father's, but there's really no pressing reason to go. You can go for a walk or sit down on her porch. In another twenty minutes she may feel differently about it.

In fact, distraction works rather well around people who are flooding. Although they may feel passionately that they must act just then, if they're briefly distracted, the whole thing might blow over. A little while later they may not even remember just why they were so upset.

So, your mother orders you out of the house, and you sit down on the front porch with a glass of iced tea. If she comes out later, you might ask her if she'd like you to wash her car. Flooding being what it is, she's entirely likely to shrug and say yes.

Similarly, if people are baiting you so that you simply can't think, you might distract them with a red herring to change the conversation and give you the chance to calm down. They may not remember to get around to bothering you again.

Here is a checklist of the mental symptoms of flooding. It's important to know which symptoms are most likely to affect you. You can check off your symptoms here, or write out a list in your notebook or journal.

Mental Symptoms Checklist

☐ Disjointed or incoherent speech, inability to get words out

☐ Jumbled or circular thinking

☐ Confusing simple everyday things, like calling your sibling by the wrong name or getting off at the wrong exit

☐ Feeling that you have no choices

☐ Feeling that you must act *now*

☐ Suggestibility

SILENT FLOODING

While some people get loud and aggressive when flooding, others become silent and withdrawn. They go inward and brace themselves against the storm of emotions they feel. Rather than act out, they may go rigid. Sometimes they're not able to get any words out. They may be every bit as upset as someone storming around the house, but their tempest is internal.

Looks can be deceiving. To the casual observer it may seem as if nothing's particularly troubling this person. In fact, the opposite is true, though other family members take offense at the quiet and try to provoke this person to get a reaction. Thinking that they're being disregarded, others may decide to give the silent one something he can't ignore. They may get more of a response than they're prepared to face.

Be aware that someone who is silently flooding is not calm, he is only silent. That volcano can blow in a hurry.

Here are the signs to recognize people who are silently flooding:

- Their faces turn red or dark.

- They are unusually still.

- They say little or nothing.

- If verbally attacked, they may not respond to defend themselves.

Rather than provoke these people, it's time to de-escalate. They're more upset than you think. Don't insist that they answer you; they may not be able to get any words out. Certainly, they aren't likely to be able to think or make sense.

Instead of provoking them, simply ask if they would like some space. If they indicate yes, then say you can talk later and leave them alone for a while. They won't be able to engage in conversation until they calm down anyway, so you may as well give them room.

If you are the type of person who silently floods, any of the normal flood control techniques described above would work for you. If you can get only one word out, try "Later." Then go for a walk. Other people need to know that you aren't ignoring them, but apart from that, you are likely to be better off somewhere else until you calm down.

HOW TO PLAN FOR FLOODING

Flooding needn't always catch you by surprise. It is a learned reaction. If you flooded the last three times you saw your stepfather, you will likely flood the next time you see him. Your body has learned that "stepfather" means flooding and it will start pumping adrenaline on cue, whether or not he says anything wrong. The mere sight of him or the sound of his voice will set your head pounding and cause your thinking to malfunction.

This learned reaction certainly can work against you, but it can also be harnessed to work in your favor. Your body can be taught to unlearn flooding, just as it learned to overreact. You do not want the mere sight of your stepfather to send you into a mental tailspin. That gives him too much power over you. You want to avoid flooding, not because you feel warm and cheerful, but because you need your brain to be able to cope.

To unlearn flooding, try the following exercise.

EXERCISE: LEARN TO PREVENT FLOODING

1. Find a quiet room where no one will interrupt you for an hour or two. Disconnect the phone. Tell the kids to turn down the TV.

2. Sit down in a comfortable chair with a pen and paper. (Bring your notebook or a separate sheet of paper.)

3. Then, conjure up the sight of whomever it is who can trigger your flooding. Visualize him or her vividly.

4. While you are imagining this person images, sounds, or smells are likely to come up for you that will particularly evoke your flooding. It may be the sound of her footsteps coming down the hall, the smirk he gets when he's made a verbal jab, or the smell of a particular cigarette. Look for these triggering cues and write down as many of them as you can recall.

5. Then, while thinking about this person and all the attending triggers, deliberately take yourself to a state of flooding. Feel it wash over you. Make note of your physical symptoms, like shortness of breath or sweaty palms.

6. Take note of your mental symptoms. Are your thoughts spinning in circles? Has your mind gone blank? Do you feel trapped? Hopeless? Write down all of your reactions.

7. Now deliberately take yourself out of flooding. Do something physical; for example, jog in place. Move your chair. Breathe deeply.

8. Once you've come back down, note your mental state. Is your mind feeling clearer? Are your thoughts steady?

9. Now, once again imagine this same upsetting person. Once again take yourself through the entire sequence. Bring yourself to the point of flooding and then bring yourself out of it again.

Doing this exercise will teach your body to disconnect the triggers and leave you better able to fend off flooding.

Ashley's Experiences with Flood Control

Here's an excellent example of one person who deliberately went into and came out of flooding.

Ashley's mom had decided to sell her house and was shopping for a place in a nicer neighborhood. However, prices were sky-high and she quickly found that she wouldn't be able to afford anything comparable to her old place. As it happened, Ashley was also thinking of buying a house, and she liked the same neighborhood her mom did. It occurred to Ashley that if they pooled their money they could buy a nice two-flat in the area they both liked. They certainly could get more house than if they bought individually.

Ashley's mom was a little hesitant about this plan, but given the price of housing they both decided it was worth a try.

They began looking at places, and Ashley's mother soon discovered that even when they pooled their money, they still couldn't afford a place as nice as the one she was leaving. This was upsetting, and the more distressed her mom got, the more upset Ashley got.

One day, Ashley was doing the driving when she realized she'd lost track of what she'd been doing and didn't really know where she was anymore. She'd been in the area dozens of times, but she couldn't get her bearings. Everything felt as if it was set to "fast forward." She felt her thoughts were crowding into her head so fast that nothing could come out.

Then she realized that her head was pounding, her palms were sweating, and her heart was racing. She was starting to stutter and mix up her words. In short, she was flooding.

Ashley could hardly talk, so she pulled the car over to the shoulder, and said, "We're flooding!" She put on the blinkers to give herself a minute. Then she rolled down the window to take some deep breaths, and kept squeezing the steering wheel as hard as she could. Meanwhile her mother was wondering if her daughter had lost her mind.

After Ashley came down a bit, she explained what she had been doing and asked if her mother had felt any of the same symptoms. Interestingly enough, Mom's symptoms were much like Ashley's, only she hadn't known what to do about them. So Mom rolled her window down and gulped some air. Coming down, they both agreed they were on adrenaline overload and decided to have dinner. Afterwards, they would make a fresh start.

In their old pattern they would have fought until they were exhausted, and then each would have stormed off. As it was, after a quiet dinner, they were able to talk about their goals, what really mattered to them both, and what they had in common. This conversation went a lot better than their previous ones, and they were able to go back to looking at houses.

Check the Guidelines

Ashley did a great many things exactly right. She may have absorbed the flooding from her mother, but she recognized her symptoms, stopped arguing, pulled herself out of it, and then got her mother to follow her example.

Here are some guidelines for handling someone else's flooding:

- Flooding is contagious, so be prepared.

- Quit arguing. The other person can't hear you anyway.

- Lower your volume. Loud voices will only raise adrenaline levels. Use a low, resonant tone of voice.

- If there's room, back up. Give the other person some space.

- If the other person is silent and tense, don't prod him. Don't try to provoke a response. This person is probably more upset than you think.

LASHING OUT AT THOSE YOU LOVE

When you're stressed out and close to flooding, you may be quick to fight with anyone around you. For example, you may be stressed about seeing your parents, so you find yourself fighting with your kids. Or your parents are coming to your house to visit, so you get into a row with your boyfriend.

You probably don't need to fight with these people. They're not the reason you're upset. The problem is that flooding has you on edge, and suddenly anyone near you feels provoking.

People who are flooding are apt to focus their anger on whomever or whatever they see at the time. We've all seen this happen in traffic jams. Cars can be backed up for miles in every direction, and someone will start honking at the car in front, just as if that one car were to blame, or as if it could levitate out of his way.

What happens is the driver has been staring at the car in front of him while his temper was heating to a boil. Soon, his fury and frustration lock onto that car, even though it's obviously not the cause of the problem.

A similar response can happen to you if you're tense about seeing your parents. For instance, let's say your kids come home from school and drop their books on the dining room table. Any other time you couldn't care less, but now you're full of adrenaline. Suddenly the sight of books on the dining room table has you furious.

Check your head, your heart rate, whatever symptoms are the most common for you. If you're flooding, leave the kids alone and take a walk. You have enough problems without fighting with your kids.

HAVE A FALLBACK PLAN

We're all hardwired for flooding. It's part of the human condition, so we can't hope to do away with it completely. Instead it's best to have a fallback plan. Think of it in three parts:

1. Know what to do to prevent flooding.

2. Know how to bring yourself out of flooding should it happen anyway.

3. If completely overwhelmed by flooding, know how to gain space until you can think clearly again.

It's best to have a plan in place so you won't have to improvise when your brain is already malfunctioning. For example, you may decide in advance that if your dad starts to criticize you and you start to flood, you will go to the garage and start moving boxes. Should the occasion arise, just nod and leave. This requires no brainpower and will protect you. Later, when your head clears, you can go back and deal with your father.

If your brother once again starts criticizing how you ran your business that failed five years ago, you can decide in advance that you will say, "That was a long time ago," and then change the subject to Aunt Maria's cat. You'll do this knowing full well that Maria will talk about her kitty for the next several hours and that, perhaps, it will drive your brother out of the house.

You don't have to use a brilliant or witty comeback. In fact, it's better that you don't. All you need to do is choose an option that is easy to remember and does no harm.

SOLUTIONS FOR FLOODING

Following are several common situations likely to inspire flooding. The accompanying suggestions provide a variety of ways you might use to handle flooding yourself.

You're driving to your parents' house and you're so upset you can hardly breathe.

- Turn on the radio and start singing at the top of your lungs. Don't bother meekly humming along with the music. Really belt it.

- Squeeze the steering wheel with both hands as hard as you can.

- Roll down the window and inhale some fresh air.

- If someone cuts you off in traffic, don't even think about bothering him. You may have things to be angry about, but don't take it out on a stranger.

- Watch your speed. When distracted by flooding it's easy to drive too fast for the conditions on the road.

- If you really can't focus, pull off to the side of the road and pound the dashboard for a while. You can get back on the road once your head is clear.

- Pull over at a rest stop, get out of the car, and walk around. Do not get more coffee or caffeine. You don't need to be any more on edge.

- If you get lost, pull over to the side of the road and breathe. Do not get into an argument with your passengers about whose fault it is. You'll probably need to calm down before you can make sense of the road map.

- If the kids start fighting in the backseat, they've probably absorbed your tension. Don't yell at them, sing at them. Get them singing, too. It will help you all to calm down.

- Don't talk on your cell phone. You're already not thinking well. Any more distraction and you could have an accident.

You walk through the door at the annual family gathering. Instead of "Hey, great to see you!" you hear, "Idiot! Don't track that mess in here!"

- Say, "I left something back in the car," and walk right back out the door. Walk up and down the steps a few times until you calm down.

- Lift your bags out of the car. Lift the car. If they're watching from the window that'll really distract them.

- Do resist the urge to carry all your packages up the stairs in a single trip. First, you could hurt yourself. Second, you're not as coordinated as you might be, and you could drop things and trip over your feet. Finally, you'll calm down faster by making multiple trips up and down the stairs.

- Don't go back to deal with them until your head's clear.

At dinner, someone makes a belittling remark. You start flooding.

- Stop eating. You won't be able to taste the food anyway, so put your fork down.

- Take a deep breath. You can get a grip on yourself without anyone noticing.

- Do isometrics: Press your arms against the arms of your chair. Slip your hands under the dinner table and lift straight up.

- If you can lift the dinner table, put it back down. You've just introduced a new line of discussion.

- Wait until your head clears before you say anything. No one will be listening anyway, so you have all the time in the world.

If someone is baiting you, say, "Actually, I was wondering about . . ." and introduce the distraction of your choice. Decide the topic in advance. Arthritis or babies can derail any discussion. By the time the conversation comes back to you, you'll have had plenty of time to collect yourself.

EXERCISE: CREATE A PLAN

Now you are ready to create your own plan for the next time you have to deal with your family. You don't need to allow for every possibility. Just create some options for yourself in case you find yourself flooding and unable to think. You can write down your plan here or in your separate notebook.

When talking to a relative on the phone and I'm convinced my head will soon explode, I will:

_____

_____

_____

_____

My friends have noticed that I become surly and quick to snap before I visit my family. Therefore, I will:

_____

_____

_____

_____

Write about a tense situation of your own here. Think about your options and decide in advance how you will choose to handle things. Write your options below or in your separate notebook.

1. If a tense situation with my family is approaching, I will prevent my flooding by:

_____

_____

_____

2. If I start flooding anyway, I will bring myself out by doing:

_____

3. If I become completely overwhelmed, I will gain space until I can clear my head by doing:

_____

_____

_____

_____

Flooding can be controlled. It may have controlled you in the past, but you can win now because of a very simple fact: you're smarter than a chemical. Adrenaline can't help what it does. You can. When adrenaline is in control, bad things happen. When you're in control, your life can be manageable again.

Chapter Two

The Conflict Continuum

Now that you have the basics of flood control, new possibilities are open to you. After all, it's hard to get along with people without a brain. We've all been there and it hasn't gone well. Now, if you like, you can handle things differently.

Next we're going to look at different kinds of conflict, because all conflicts do not follow the same dynamics. We'll start by exploring the kind of conflict that happens inside your family.

The following quiz is based on my own model, which was first described in *Conflict Unraveled: Fixing Problems at Work and in Families* (Medea 2004). These questions will help you to benchmark the kind of conflicts happening around you.

When you answer the questions, please concentrate on the primary person who concerns you. Of course, your entire family may concern you but try to picture the family member who inspired you to pick up this book. Think of how that person behaves and how you behave around him or her. Then answer the questions by being as fair, honest, and objective as is possible. I know—it's hard to be objective when someone ticks you off. But give it a try.

Choose the answer that is most true about you and this other person. Either circle the number below or write it down in your notebook.

QUIZ: YOUR FAMILY'S FIGHTING STYLE

When we disagree:

1. We genuinely respect and listen to each other.

2. Sharp words may be spoken, or people may silently seethe, but then we settle down and work things out.

3. Things get extreme when we argue. We don't listen, and if we settle down, it's only a matter of time before things blow up again.

4. When we argue, I feel physically in danger.

When times get hard:

1. We bring out the best in each other.

2. We tend to give each other a tough time and then get past it.

3. Times stay hard. Improvements don't seem to last.

4. If tension gets high, I think about my safety or the safety of the kids.

When we disagree:

1. I feel the other person is still being fair.

2. The other person might get rigid, but will later cool down and become more balanced.

3. There's no dealing with this person. It's his way or the highway.

4. I feel in physical danger.

Although we disagree:

1. It still feels like we're on solid ground.

2. Getting the simplest thing done is like wading through thick mud.

3. Dealing with this person feels like being caught in quicksand. The harder I struggle, the worse things get.

4. If I don't want to get hurt, I'll just give in.

When this person gets mad:

1. He tries hard not to hurt my feelings.

2. She'll get mad over inconsequential things.

3. He can do real emotional damage.

4. I work hard not to let this person get mad. I'm afraid of her temper.

When this person fights:

1. She fights fair: there's no name calling, no taking unfair advantage.

2. He will say things he'll regret later.

3. She has to win or there'll be trouble.

4. Once he gets mad, he can't stop. It's frightening.

When I'm around this person:

1. It's easy to relax. I feel safe.

2. She's fine unless she's mad. Then it's best to wait until she cools down.

3. Whether I relax or try really hard, nothing really seems to get better.

4. I can't relax around this person. I always keep an ear out for trouble.

This person:

1. Really works at being fair.

2. Is fair unless something sets him off.

3. To her, "fair" only means she's right.

4. "Fair" is whatever he wants, at any cost.

This person:

1. Sets clear, reasonable boundaries.

2. Might step on my toes at times, but then we thrash it out and we're okay.

3. Gets mean or guilt trips me when things don't go his way.

4. Gets dangerous, so I try not to cross her.

In the general course of things, this person:

1. Levels with me.

2. Can turn on the charm when he wants something.

3. Is so manipulative I can't imagine her being square with me.

4. Is so different around other people, it's like Dr. Jekyll and Mr. Hyde.

When I really need to talk to my family:

1. I can talk with them and work things out.

2. They can be hard to deal with, but once they know something's really important they'll drop their routines and listen to me.

3. I can object as much as I want, but it doesn't get me anywhere.

4. I don't even tell my friends what goes on with my family.

In general:

1. My family talks through problems and solves them.

2. My family might start by blaming each other or refusing to face facts. Then they'll settle down and solve the problem.

3. Even when we talk, nothing ever gets solved. Problems just go on and on.

4. If I talked honestly, someone would go to jail.

In our usual way of dealing with each other:

1. We're pretty open and straightforward with each other.

2. We might take jabs or try to manipulate each other, but eventually we'll get around to talking turkey.

3. Our lives are made up of hidden jabs and manipulations—or open jabs, for that matter.

4. Even if this person is nice to other people, he can be vicious to me.

As we work through situations:

1. As a family, we're good at give-and-take.

2. As a family, we'll do give-and-take only if anger and manipulation don't work.

3. Give-and-take has no real meaning around here. Anger and manipulation rule.

4. We make threats to get what we want.

In coping with this person:

1. I deal with her pretty easily.

2. He can be a handful at times.

3. It exhausts me to deal with him.

4. I can't deal with her. I wall myself away even if I need help.

When it really comes down to it:

1. I can trust this person to do what's best.

2. He may be a pain at first, but eventually he'll do what's best.

3. She'll do what's best for herself. Everybody else had better watch out.

4. His idea of doing what's best can put someone in the hospital.

When it comes to doing what's fair:

1. My family members are decent people with a fair grasp of right and wrong.

2. It's more important for them to be right than to do right.

3. Right and wrong got lost a long time ago around here.

4. If nobody knows, then nobody gets hurt.

After the worst is over:

1. We talk, maybe joke around, or go out for coffee.

2. The fight's over, but I still think about good comebacks.

3. The worst is never over. A new fight's always just around the corner.

4. We don't talk about our fights, and I don't tell other people. No one would believe me.

Scoring

Now, add up how many times you circled "1," "2," "3," or "4." Please write down your totals for each category. Take a fresh page in your journal to record your answers there. You can do this easily by using the format below:

1, _____ 2, _____ 3, _____ 4, _____.

When you finish adding up your score, move on to the second part of the quiz just below:

If there's a history of physical violence from this person, apart from childhood spats, add 10 points to category 4.

If there has ever been sexual abuse from this person, add 20 points to category 4.

If there is drug or alcohol abuse that has resulted in physical injury or damage to anyone's health, add 10 points to category 4.

If there is drug or alcohol use that has damaged relationships or caused job problems, but has not resulted in physical harm, add 10 points to category 3.

© Copyright, Andra Medea 2004

What Your Scores Mean

If the majority of your answers are 1's, then your conflicts are primarily at Level One, problem-solving. If the majority of your answers are 2's, then your main concern is Level Two, power plays or psychological warfare. If the majority of your answers are 3's, then the issues for you are in Level Three, that is, third-degree conflict, or blind behavior. Finally, if your highest score is made up of 4's, then you need to be concerned about Level Four or predatory behavior or tyranny.

Now, with your scores in mind, please look over the Conflict Continuum.

YOUR FAMILY ON THE CONFLICT CONTINUUM CHART

Dr. Virginia Hoffman of Loyola University taught my model in a class on family dynamics. Since she had to explain it to many students, she came up with concise and interesting ways to summarize it. As she put it, when conflict is at Level One: Problem-Solving, we largely say and do things that make sense. Our actions may not be cheerful or enlightened, but they're still basically rational (Hoffman 2005).

By Level Two: Power Plays, we start to say and do things that really don't make sense. For the moment we forget about solving anything, we just want to beat down or outwit the other person. Fortunately, in this range, eventually, we're able to get over ourselves, clean up our behavior, and go back to solving problems.

By Level Three: Blind Behavior, we say and do things we would never say or do if we were thinking clearly. Far from solving the problem, we just make things worse. The situation is dysfunctional; our best efforts only dig us in deeper. Like the codependent who tries to get an alcoholic to stop drinking, we can struggle mightily and still be mystified at how bad things get. Sometimes, we stop struggling completely because it has become painfully obvious that our efforts aren't working.

By Level Four: Predation or Tyranny, our behavior is so out of control that we have become a danger to ourselves and those around us.

MEDEA'S CONFLICT CONTINUUM

NORMAL RANGE

FIRST-DEGREE CONFLICT: PROBLEM-SOLVING	SECOND-DEGREE CONFLICT: POWER PLAYS or PSYCHOLOGICAL WARFARE
Healthy Conflict	**Unhealthy Conflict**
Conflict on solid ground	Conflict as morass
Rational, makes sense	Seemingly irrational, senseless
Exercise of self-control	Lack of control; overkill
Appropriate behavior	Inappropriate behavior
Reasonable grasp of reality	Difficulties with reality; denial
Appropriate boundaries	Invasion of boundaries
Pays attention to facts, info	Withholds facts or information
Stable, even boring	False charm, flattery
Prefers a clean fight; able to negotiate	Accusation, manipulation, or whining; loss of negotiation
Flexibility	Rigidity
Pursues an end to conflict	Conflict endless; reignites
Relatively stoic	Self-pity/self-righteousness
Can live with other opinions	Crazy-making; crazyland starts here

MEDEA'S CONFLICT CONTINUUM

INCREASINGLY ABNORMAL RANGE

THIRD-DEGREE CONFLICT: BLIND BEHAVIOR/ DYSFUNCTION	FOURTH-DEGREE CONFLICT: PREDATION or TYRANNY
Increasingly unhealthy conflict	**Very unhealthy conflict**
Conflict as quicksand	Conflict as undertow
Oblivious to own behavior	Malice, vengeance
Extreme overreaction	Rage seizures/violence
Outrageous passed as normal	Felonies
Believes own lies	Forces others to lie for him/her
Missing boundaries	Bell jar effect
Sweeps issues under rug	Treacherous secrets
Highly charming/convincing	Jekyll and Hyde behavior
Bullying; hidden, often dormant, ability to negotiate	Abuse with charm; baiting the trap
Dysfunctional patterns:	**All abuse systems:**
Early-stage addiction	Late-stage addiction
Racism, homophobia, or religious intolerance	Hatred/blood feuds
	Sexual abuse
Symptoms often seen in victims first:	
Numb or participatory behavior	Learned helplessness
Failure to act in own interest	Tendency to react in extremes: either doormat or explosive
Decayed sense of justice	

Source: Conflict Unraveled: Fixing Problems at Work and in Families.

How to Use the Chart

Although characteristics change from column to column, basically behavior deteriorates. The traits keep getting worse. For instance, a degree of stoicism at Level One gives way to self-pity and self-righteousness at Level Two. There's no comparable line at Levels Three and Four, since space is limited and English doesn't have words that describe ever-increasing self-pity or self-righteousness.

But consider someone so blind to his own behavior that he doesn't even notice the damage around him. Seeing no problem, such people are apt to be profoundly sure of themselves no matter how wrongheaded they are, and they feel greatly aggrieved if someone calls them on it. ("Quit telling me to stop drinking! I'm fine, dammit! The only reason I drink is because of you!") Finally, the tyrants and predators at Level Four can be downright sanctimonious, heaping guilt and shame on their victims even as they abuse them.

There is a danger with reading this chart. It's altogether too tempting to place everyone we dislike at the difficult, extreme end of the chart, and put our own noble selves at Level One. But life is not so simple.

These forms of conflict are infectious. They're every bit as contagious as flooding. If your sister baits you over dinner, she's obviously operating in an unhealthy range. If you take the bait and lash out over the creamed peas, then you've crossed into unhealthy conflict yourself. Unless you have been through many years of successful therapy, you must assume that if your relatives are operating in an unhealthy category, you'll be drawn in, too.

Even in an ideal family, once you start flooding, you can expect to cross over into power plays or blind behavior. Your temper's up, your brain is spinning, and you long to give someone a piece of your mind. You may think you're being rational, even when a vein starts pulsing above your left eye. But where do you think you'll end up? Probably someplace regrettable.

The other part of the continuum to note is that blind behavior and tyranny or predation have special sets of characteristics for victims. This behavior is so extreme that it can't be shrugged off. It causes lasting damage.

For instance, a family that's suffered from domestic violence has a string of predictable symptoms. Family members often fail to act in their own interest, making excuses for the abuser or covering up for the alcoholic. They often become numb. Shocking behavior fails to shock them. They have such "battle fatigue" that threats or even beatings hardly spark a reaction. It's not that the victims don't care. It's that numbing themselves became their working defense. They have given up trying to protect themselves, and consequently they may fail to react at all.

More dangerous yet, victims in the deeply unhealthy range may display participatory behavior. For example, they may help Uncle Larry get his vodka, or they may provoke Mom when she's becoming dangerous in order to lure her away from a younger sibling.

These are not ordinary, everyday traits; they are the fallout from deeply disturbing patterns. If your family has or had these problems, you have serious work ahead of you. Your own behavior may have mystified you at times. You may have wondered why you put up with these things, or what was wrong with your mind that you did put up with them. Actually, you were behaving normally within an abnormal system.

CONFLICTS AT THE DIFFERENT LEVELS

Let's look at some examples to clarify the idea that different kinds of conflict operate by different rules. Let's say you and your sister are pretty decent to each other even when you fight. You leave some space for compromise and even listen to each other when things go wrong. You may not exactly like each other at that moment and your patience may start to wear thin, but you do your level best to work things out. That's problem-solving at Level One.

However, no one's perfect, and let's say your patience gives way. You and your sister have a temporary flare-up. Perhaps you're both visiting your folks for the holidays, and after that you've made plans to visit an old friend, but you discover your sister is about to go off with the family car. You react: "Hey! Not so fast! I'm supposed to get the car." You both dig in your heels and try to face each other down, but neither of you give in. After a little while, you realize this won't get either of you out of the house, so you start bargaining about how the car can be shared, who can be dropped off where, and how you can get a lift back home. You both blew up, realized it wouldn't get you anywhere, and then finally settled down and solved the problem.

That's Level Two: a foray into psychological warfare. However, you then drop the foolishness and get back to business.

But let's say you and your sister have a sour relationship, with chronic patterns of things going wrong between the two of you. You no sooner see each other than you regress to the kind of nasty jabs and sniping you both did when you were angry adolescents. You won't compromise about the car or anything else. You re-create enough old patterns and open enough old wounds to leave both of you angry and wishing you'd never come home. Together, you both manage to ruin the visit for yourselves and those around you. That's Level Three: Blind Behavior, a chronic, debilitating, and ultimately miserable form of conflict.

Finally, Level Four predation might occur when both you and your sister encounter an uncle who was just released from jail for child molesting. You both have your own memories of the man, and, frankly, you hate him. He's very charming and behaves as if he's just come back from an extended business trip. No one in the family mentions where he's been. You and your sister both grow silent and watchful as he plays with a young cousin, and yet you do nothing. You leave feeling troubled, upset, and vaguely ill.

It's easy to freeze in the presence of a predator, but it's not logical and is not a useful survival skill. It's evidence of the old traps that still bind you.

You and your sister are not predators, but you've both fallen into a classic victim role. You become strangely passive around someone you fear and detest. You fail to act in your own interest, or in the interest of the vulnerable child. The entire scene makes you feel ill, yet you do nothing.

Of course, this does not make you as bad as the predator or somehow complicit in his crimes. It does show you how you can fall into predictable patterns that can be understood and prevented.

Knowledge means freedom. In the past you were caught in these conflict patterns because you didn't know what they were. Once you see how they work, you can learn to change them.

EXERCISE: YOUR FAMILY AND HEALTHY CONFLICT

Now, think over the characteristics of healthy conflict. Here's a list to refresh your memory:

- A solid feel to the conflict

- Fairly rational behavior (Expecting all parties to be totally rational is a tall order.)

- Even in a bad mood, self-control still evident

- Behavior and reactions appropriate to the occasion

- A willingness to cope with reality and not ignore it

- Responsive to facts and information

- A minimum of drama involved (Behavior may even be on the edge of boring.)

- A clean fight (avoiding name-calling, low shots, or manipulation)

- The use of negotiation rather than force

- Flexibility, a certain amount of give-and-take

- Relatively stoical behavior

- Can live with differences, rather than try to suppress them

Even the worst family has its healthy moments. Now, think about a time when you and someone else from your family handled a problem while acting this way. You may not have even noticed this was conflict, because it seemed like just working things out.

After you come up with a memory, take out your journal or notebook and briefly describe the situation you experienced that qualifies as Level One, that is, at problem-solving.

Thinking back, what were your feelings at the time? How do you feel looking back at it? Some feelings people have reported experiencing in Level One conflicts are self-respect, courage, strength, healing, or even happiness. Happiness may be an odd feeling to report in terms of conflict, but that or other unexpected emotions may come up during healthy conflicts.

Now, list some of the feelings you remember from that conflict in your journal.

EXERCISE: YOUR FAMILY AND UNHEALTHY CONFLICT

Now, think about the characteristics of power plays or psychological warfare that are found at Level Two. Here is a list to refresh your memory:

- Conflict like a morass

- Seemingly irrational or senseless

- Lack of control, overkill

- Inappropriate behavior

- Difficulties with reality, or denial

- Invading each others' boundaries

- Withholding facts or information

- False charm or flattery

- Angry accusations that may or may not be true

- Whining

- Rigidity

- Superior attitude or belittling behavior

- Conflict reignites

- Self-pity

- Self-righteousness

- Both sides don't listen, become deaf to input

Now, think of a time when you and another family member fell into some of these behaviors. In your notebook or journal, briefly describe the situation that qualified as Level Two: power plays or psychological warfare.

Thinking back, what were your feelings at Level Two, when you or others were engaged in a power struggle or psychological warfare?

Some feelings people have reported experiencing at this level are misery, depression, boredom, low self-esteem, anxiety, frustration, or hopelessness. Some reported a temporary high, or a sense of satisfaction, that plummeted when they later realized the situation was falling apart.

Now, list some of the feelings you remember from that conflict in your journal or notebook.

The next chapters will cover these different types of conflict in depth. We'll talk about the kinds of patterns that arise, along with the best ways of handling these patterns.

Chapter Three

Healthy and Unhealthy Conflict

This chapter will cover the first two levels of ordinary conflict, columns one and two on the Conflict Continuum Chart in chapter 2. Why cover both together? Because these two styles together are where everyday life takes place.

Normal people aren't saints practicing dazzlingly healthy behavior at all times. Every once in a while, the nicest, healthiest people slip up and veer into unhealthy behavior. Perhaps they're in a bad mood, or too hungry, or maybe just stuck in traffic. But whatever the reason may be, at least once in a while we all act out around our nearest and dearest. This doesn't mean we have an evil streak. It means we're human.

For those of you who have always wondered what "normal" looks like, this is how normal works. It's not about perfection. It's about ordinary people slipping up and making mistakes, then settling down, and getting back on track.

People don't necessarily haul themselves back to better behavior because they're feeling good, cheerful, or magnanimous. They may pull themselves together while in a rotten, surly mood. The main reason they do this is because healthy behavior is really the only way problems ever get sorted out. They may also have the vague realization that the people around them deserve better.

This is how everyday problems get solved: people get annoyed, veer into the unhealthy territory charted in chapter two, then stop, catch themselves, and do better. The point at which they return to healthy behavior is the point at which their conflict turns around. In this range, matters are fixed by a move back to problem-solving.

So, should you slip up, you can do the same: pull yourself together, make apologies where needed, and go back to the behaviors outlined in column one. This is the benchmark for sensible living. This will keep your family on course. Below is your plan for everyday conflict.

EVERYDAY CONFLICT

The all-too-normal range of conflicts includes:

- Everyday mishaps

- Miscommunications

- Temporary ups and downs

Normal levels of conflict do *not* include:

- Chronic, damaging family patterns

- Addictions or psychiatric disorders

- Hatefulness or bigotry

- Revenge

- Emotional, physical, or sexual abuse

In short, this chapter will cover ordinary conflict that can pop up in any family on any given day. If everyday behavior in your family of origin includes revenge, addictions, or physical violence, then your major conflicts are still to come. Nonetheless, you might read this chapter with an eye for how regular people deal with ordinary problems; it will most likely benefit you.

The thing to remember is that problem-solving behavior does, in fact, solve problems. Power plays and psychological warfare rarely solve anything and will usually compound the problem.

Your goal, therefore, is to learn to spot different traits and recognize when things are veering out of control or going astray. These important benchmarks can keep you on the path of problem-solving.

HOW HEALTHY CONFLICT WORKS

Let's say your parents come to visit you because they want to take your four- and seven-year-old kids to Disneyland. However, you think the kids are too young for such a long trip, and your parents don't know what they're getting themselves into.

Your parents may be disappointed that you say no. If your kids happen to overhear, they won't be pleased with you either. But both sides are sane and understandable, even if they make things uncomfortable for you. If there's a meltdown, it will be caused by your kids acting like kids, not your parents acting juvenile.

You may be in for some tough bargaining, as both your parents and kids try to talk you out of your decision. You may work out a compromise: The kids can go, but you or your partner has to come along to help keep order. Or your parents can take the kids on a day-trip to a water park this summer. If that goes well, the kids can go to Disneyland next year when they're older.

This compromise reflects the appropriate boundaries. You, the parent, have the final say. Everyone faces the facts. It may be unrealistic to think a four-year-old can handle a long trip, but a day at a water park could be fine. You discuss the situation openly and settle the problem through negotiation. Finally, you all want the problem to be over. No one wants to rehash this during every phone call throughout the year.

It's a genuine conflict, but the family manages to work it out with a minimum of hurt feelings and disappointment. Even though some— or all—don't get what they want, everyone can live with the results. The family as a whole probably will come away from this conflict with more respect for each other for having thrashed it through fairly.

That is what healthy conflict looks like. But, of course, that's not what families always do.

Close-Up on Healthy Conflict

Healthy conflict focuses on the problem: how best to take young kids on a long trip. During this conflict the adults more or less stay realistic. (By the way, it isn't a child's job to be realistic. That's for adults.) Adjustments are made. People try to be flexible, even when they'd really prefer to have their own way. Boundaries are respected.

The adults cope in a relatively stoic fashion when things don't work out as they'd envisioned. The kids may not cope as stoically, since they're not as mature, but they will take their cues from the adults. Grown-ups bargain for a compromise and one is worked out. The situation stabilizes relatively quickly. Everyone grows from the experience and the family moves on.

HOW UNHEALTHY CONFLICT WORKS

Let's take the same situation played out in unhealthy ways. Your parents don't start by first talking with you; instead, they bring up the Disneyland trip in front of your kids. That's pushing your boundaries, bypassing you as the parent. Once the kids are eager and screaming to go, your parents smile and look at you as if it's a done deal. That's manipulation. That puts you in the position of either capitulating when you don't think it's a good idea, or crushing your children's happiness and living with whining for the next two weeks.

Thoroughly annoyed—and flooding—you snap at your parents for setting you up. Caught short, and not at your best, you say inappropriate things in front of the kids. Now you've exhibited accusatory behavior, overkill, and your own invasion of boundaries.

At this point, your parents, who perhaps knew they were trying to pull a fast one, become self-righteously indignant. Of course they're flooding as well, and they act out accordingly. They leave in a huff and are short with you for weeks. In retaliation for their punishing you for acting like a parent, and tired of them hardly speaking to you, you're tempted not to tell them that little Jimmy will be making his debut at a

Little League game. Discarding that idea, you think about not mentioning it until shortly before the game, knowing that it'll be inconvenient for them to get there on short notice. So, now, you are the one ready to manipulate and withhold information.

You teeter on the brink, mulling over this sneaky plan—and then snap out of it. This is their grandkid. They have a right to be at Jimmy's game, and besides, you'd never hear the end of it. So you get over yourself and call to tell them about it.

You come very close to doing something that could really damage the relationship, then you stop, and change course. By doing this you've avoided a family rupture and set your family back on the course to healthy conflict.

If you allowed it to go on, it's likely you would descend into the endless chronic fighting and manipulation of dysfunctional behavior. However, somewhere around this point most healthy families will sense that things have gone far enough and they will start to correct their behavior. If you won't budge, your partner can call and mention Little League. The grandparents will stop sulking about the trip and talk about baseball. Both sides ease their way back into contact because, after all, they would rather have the fight end.

The adults don't make this effort because they feel cheerful, warm, or that all is well. They do it in order to save themselves.

Close-Up on Unhealthy Conflict

Unhealthy conflict is more invested in winning than in merely solving a problem. In the second example, your parents became inappropriate and, for that matter, so did you. First there was manipulation, then flooding fueled the breakdown. People got mean, and said inappropriate things. This second conflict became a power struggle over the kids. The driving force was to come out on top, even while family members got their feelings hurt.

Ordinary rules became skewed. Boundaries were violated as your parents worked on your kids. Instead of compromising, both sides became rigid. Both sides stopped listening and became deaf to input. Both sides withheld information as part of the power play; your parents about their plans and you about Jimmy's sports debut. Everyone, no doubt, felt heartily sorry for themselves. If you had been able to call a temporary truce, the conflict would have reignited very easily.

What might have been a pleasant family exchange turned into a morass. Crazyland starts here. Yet once the adults decide this conflict has gone far enough, the family can change course and go back to a healthier form of behavior. All is not well, but the adults are able to work things out.

Now let's look at how these traits play out.

RATIONAL AS OPPOSED TO IRRATIONAL

Healthy conflict tends to make sense, even if it isn't pleasant. Anger and upset tend to be proportional. For instance, suppose your Uncle Mark spills red wine on your new couch. Flooding, you hit the ceiling.

The intensity of conflict will depend on the severity of the problem: for instance, the conflict will get better if you can get the stain out or if your Uncle Mark apologizes. The conflict will get worse if your uncle stands there smirking, or if he turns around and spills salsa on your rug.

None of this is pleasant or comfortable, but your anger does make sense.

Unhealthy conflict really doesn't make sense. Power plays can erupt over nothing at all. At Level Two, a family can get into a furious fight about how to pop popcorn or who grows better tomatoes.

Popping popcorn needn't be so emotionally loaded that it derails a family event. Normally, adults are flexible enough to handle popcorn-making without getting into a fight about whose way is "right." Also, families are normally forgiving enough that they can deal with unpopped kernels without resorting to nasty taunts. They simply aren't needed.

Self-Control as Opposed to Overkill

In every family, people have to bite their tongue at times to keep the peace. You could weigh in with your opinion about your father's new girlfriend, who puts your teeth on edge. But you don't. You know it would upset him and only drive them closer together, so you take a deep breath and find something pleasant to say.

Everyone "loses it" sometimes, but in a healthy family there's a real effort not to go too far. Moreover, self-control has cultural norms, and self-control in a raucous Sicilian family is different from self-control in a staid British household. But all families have their own unwritten codes about going too far. Healthy families are respectful of others and individuals in healthy families do what they can to stay within bounds.

Even so, we all face situations where we're not sure how to react. At such times, we avoid lashing out if only because that will make matters worse.

Let's say you arrive at a family picnic. You've agreed to bring a vegetable, so you've put together a nice salad made with chicken. Your brother brings his new date. He neglected to mention she's a vegetarian.

Now your brother is annoyed with you because his date can't eat your salad. You're annoyed with him because you easily could have put the chicken on the side, if only he'd told you. His date is embarrassed because this is the first time she's met you and already she's the cause of contention. Besides, there isn't much for her to eat besides some Cheetos.

Everyone is stressed and has problems to work out. Your brother needs to be more forthcoming, so you can plan better in the future. You need to not take it personally that his date won't eat your salad, and you probably need to cope with your feelings of chagrin. You also need to talk to his date despite this tense moment, because she's a guest and needs to feel welcomed. It's certainly not a time to lecture her on her eating habits.

Everyone, hopefully, will struggle with their self-control. No one gets to throw a fit. So you quietly gnash your teeth, take your brother aside for a quiet word, and try to think of what to feed the girlfriend.

Interested in Facts/Difficulties with Reality

People engaged in problem-solving deal well with facts. They might prefer that other things were true, but they'll deal with facts as they are. Your brother's date is a vegetarian. That's a fact. Don't try to feed her salami.

Once people cross the line into power plays, they take a more ingenious approach to facts. For example, it's unhealthy to think that your brother's date should eat your chicken salad, because you made it and you will not be made to look like a piker.

During power plays, reality becomes optional.

For instance, one daughter had just completed a sane discussion about real estate with her father, when she got on the phone with her mom. Getting nowhere talking buildings, the daughter, against her own better judgment, mentioned that she had just had some basal skin cancer cells removed. Without losing a beat, her mother asked her if it was really skin cancer, and then informed her that she shouldn't be spending any more money.

This could make you wonder whether Mom isn't due for psychological testing, until you notice the sheer practicality of it all. Mom is essentially faced with two choices:

- Plan A: face facts, or

- Plan B: prove she's in charge of this conversation and in control of the family

Plan B won.

Listening as Opposed to Deaf to Input

Another aspect of Mom's not registering skin cancer is that she has become deaf to input. Some people become impervious to facts. This leads to all sorts of fascinating family dialogues:

- "Dad, I'm gay."

- "You are not."

This time, of all times, would be ideal for some listening skills, along with a little self-control, and the ability to face facts. Depending on Dad's attitude, some flood control could also be in order. Flatly refusing to listen is not particularly useful.

APPROPRIATE AS OPPOSED TO INAPPROPRIATE BEHAVIOR

Appropriate behavior can be tricky in a family, because, by its very nature, a family grows and changes. One kind of conduct is appropriate with a child, and a different kind of conduct is appropriate with an adult. It's appropriate to tell a child to bundle up before going outside. It can be insulting to say that to a twenty-six-year-old man.

Appropriate behavior also includes common courtesy. For instance, if the family agrees to sit down to dinner together, then they should show up on time and turn off their cell phones. Other appropriate behaviors include showing due respect, helping in appropriate rather than condescending ways, and being civil to one another.

When families' behaviors become inappropriate, they can be not only rude but sometimes breathtakingly so. For instance, suppose you've just come back from the kitchen, and you bring your brother a beer.

Appropriate response: "Thank you."

Inappropriate response: "You know, waitressing really suits you."

This is psychological warfare. Your brother not only belittles you and embarrasses you in front of others, but laughing, he gets to deny his comment was anything but a joke.

There's a good deal of difference between appropriate and inappropriate humor. Appropriate humor is pleasant and bonding. Inappropriate humor is belittling and hostile. Inappropriate humor encourages others to laugh at your expense. Of course, if you're flooding, you wouldn't have a snappy comeback and might be inclined to pour the beer on his head. At that point, though, your behavior would have become as inappropriate as his was.

A more appropriate course, if you didn't hear "Thank you," might be to turn around and bring the beer back into the kitchen. It would make your point and would still require considerable self-control.

Negotiation as Opposed to Accusation, Manipulation, or Whining

When a family is focused on problem-solving they often fall back on negotiation. Petty concerns are set aside while they work out ways to make things go smoothly.

Here are some examples of negotiation statements:

- "Look, could we just start over?"

- "What if we tried . . ."

- "You know, we're both tired. Why don't we talk about this in the morning?"

- "Maybe we could agree to disagree."

The key factor in negotiation is that the other person is trying to work things out with you. She doesn't necessarily say the things you want to hear. She doesn't flatter you, and is not especially cheerful. Frankly, she may have had enough of you for now and is trying for a civil exit. But as tired as she is, she's signaled that the two of you can coexist peacefully and she wants to stop fighting. Or perhaps she's still willing to thrash things out, just later, in a kinder fashion.

Once family members cross over into unhealthy conflict, negotiation is forgotten and a different set of skills appears. The first of these is the use of accusation or belligerence. Rather than come up with an offer, they attack.

Here are some examples of accusation or belligerence:

- "As if you knew the meaning of hard work."

- "You call that dinner? I call it dog food."

- "Trying to be a big shot are you? Trying to show how smart you are."

- "You're telling me your car made it all the way here? Did you push it?"

Notice how easily humor can be used to disguise belligerence. But if humor makes someone smaller, it isn't really funny. It's just mean.

Belligerence can be shown in lots of ways: shoving furniture, slamming the door, even a compliment said in a nasty tone of voice. Similarly, an accusation may not be directed against you. It may insult your spouse, date, dog, or the present you brought for Grandpa's birthday.

The next skill of psychological warfare is manipulation. Even when there's a simple and straightforward way to get something done, family members use guilt and underhanded tactics to gain an advantage.

Here are some examples of manipulation:

- "If you really cared about this family, you would . . ."

- "Don't you want to be liked?"

- "Do you want to upset your mother?"

- "But I'm only thinking of you."

Families can be extraordinarily good at manipulation. Of course, they know all your buttons; they installed them. Yet these "hot buttons" may be arbitrary. For instance, you may feel shame at the mention of not being good enough for your own flesh and blood. In another family, that might rate only a puzzled stare. Or your family may evoke waves of guilt when you've slighted a sit-down dinner. Other families may have no strong feelings about sit-down dinners, and never think to feel distressed if you weren't there.

The last skill of unhealthy conflict is whining, or playing the victim. Whining is certainly a skill. With some people it's nearly an art form.

Here are some examples of whining or playing the victim:

- "Why am I always the last to know?"

- "Sure, that's easy for you to say."

- "Would it be too hard to show a little consideration?"

- "Look, I don't like to borrow money, but you were the one with all the breaks."

- "Not everyone can have a great car like you do."

- "It's not like I'm asking for anything special . . ."

- "Is it really asking for so much . . ."

- "I could be dead for all you'd care."

The odd thing about whining is that it may mask a perfectly normal request. Your dad may want you to move your car because you're blocking the driveway. There's nothing wrong with that. But instead of just asking, your dad says, "Is it too much for you to remember that someone else might want to use the driveway?" Now he's a victim and you'll feel an urge to defend yourself. You may slam out of the house when you go to move your car, which is a show of belligerence. Or you may whine back: "You'd think after I came all this way . . ."

Either way, now you're using unfair tactics in return, and the simple act of moving the car turns into psychological warfare.

SOLUTIONS: MOVING TO HEALTHY CONFLICT

Healthy conflict skills include many of the things we've already discussed: flood control, setting healthy boundaries, appropriate behavior, and self-control. When tempted to blow up or manipulate your family in return, you can opt for a healthier skill instead.

Let's say your mother approaches you after dinner with this request: "While you're here, could you talk to your dad about getting your sister a new car? Be a sweetie. You know he'll listen to you."

That's manipulation. Your sister's thirty-seven years old. She can arrange for her own car loans.

Here are the old ways you might have handled your mom's request:

- Go along and feel embarrassed.

- Weasel out of it somehow.

- Promise you'll do it, then conveniently forget.

- Whine to your mom about your loser sister, and *then* capitulate or weasel out of it.

Instead, try setting clear, healthy boundaries:

- "Sorry, Mom. That's not my style."

- "You know I'm really uncomfortable with this. It's time Sis talked to him herself."

- "It's not for me to get in the middle."

- Finally, if you just can't face things yet, you can retreat until you're better prepared: "Look at the time! Gotta go!"

The last choice isn't a great solution, but it may be all you can do for the moment.

Examples of Healthy Conflict

Here are a variety of situations where you can see healthy ways to handle ordinary family conflicts.

Problem

Your mother makes a slighting remark about your partner.

Solutions

Flood Control—Talk with her while you're working on something, perhaps washing the dishes or putting away packages. Breathe deeply and work those muscles.

Setting Good Boundaries—"Mom, this is someone I love. If you can't be civil, I can't sit here and listen."

Negotiation—"If this is a bad time, we can talk later. But you have to know I'm serious about this."

Problem

Your dad belittles your car.

Solutions

Flood Control—Breathe. Make a joke about great wrecks you have known.

Setting Good Boundaries—"Sounds like a good time to change the subject. How's the home team doing this year?"

Negotiation—"I've gotten fond of how the car looks, Dad, but if you'd like to help me do the body work, I've got some free time next weekend."

Problem

Your brother wants to borrow money—again.

Solutions

Flood Control—Ask him to walk with you while you talk. Go outside where you won't feel hemmed in.

Setting Good Boundaries—Say to him, "Actually, I'm not comfortable making more loans."

Negotiation—"Loans are out, but what if you came over to paint my garage? I have some money budgeted for that. What do you think?"

Problem

Your sister complains about her latest boyfriend.

Solutions

Flood Control—Stand up and move around. Stretch. You don't have to be on edge. You can relax while you listen.

Setting Good Boundaries—Remember this is her life, not yours. It's her place to work it out. It's only for you to listen: "Sis, I bet you can handle him. How did you handle the last one, anyway?"

Negotiation—"You know, I'm only going to be here a little while more. Why don't we go back downstairs? I'd like to check in with Dad before I go."

Problem

Your mom wants more time from you, and there are other people you need to see.

Solutions

Flood Control—Breathe. Break out of the circular loop of voices in your head telling you that she'll never be satisfied.

Setting Good Boundaries—"Mom, I really love you, but this just isn't a good time."

Negotiation—"Now isn't good, but what if we go bowling/garage "saling"/take in the flower show next weekend? We could make it just the two of us."

EXERCISE: HANDLING UNHEALTHY CONFLICT

Now you try it. Remember a conflict with your family that had all or some of the traits that characterize unhealthy conflict. (A conflict with all the healthy traits would probably have been solved by now.) Then, take out your journal or notebook and briefly describe the situation.

Now, think of how you might use flood control instead of veering into unhealthy behavior. For example, instead of becoming sarcastic, you could take a deep breath and press your arms firmly against the side of your chair.

Now, write down your flood control solution in your notebook.

Think about how you might set a clear boundary. (*Example:* "Sorry, Dad, but I can't do that. I have plans for tonight.")

Write down your boundary solution in your notebook or journal.

Finally, think of how you might negotiate within this situation. For instance, if someone makes an unfair demand, instead of fuming, say, "Okay, I'll run your errands while I'm out, if you're willing to help me out in the garage."

Write out your negotiation approach in your journal or notebook.

Now, if this or a similar conflict comes up again, you have three different solutions you might try. Choose the one that seems best at the time.

WE ALL GO OFF-KILTER SOMETIMES

Of course, we all like to think that we engage only in healthy conflict. But the reality is that pressure, or flooding, or unfair tactics can send anyone of us veering into the unhealthy range.

We all move easily back and forth between these first two levels of conflict. An irritable word, a sharp glance, a touch of flooding, and you might resort to power plays or to a touch of psychological warfare. (Exasperated, the cry goes up: "Oh Mom! Not again!") Then, a kind look, a reassuring word, and you will settle down and move back to problem-solving.

You may regularly flood and overreact to your eldest sister, plunging you both into power plays. Then, you may go for a ride with your youngest brother, have a few laughs, and listen to the radio. Now you're flexible and calm, ready for levelheaded sanity.

You may have been in the company of these two different people only ten minutes apart. With one you were irritable and sharp, with the other you were flexible and easygoing. Now that you know more about how conflict works, you can be more in control of your behavior and state of mind, and not be as vulnerable to the bad moods of others.

You needn't plunge into unhealthy behavior just because someone in your family feels the urge to yank your chain. Your behavior becomes yours to control.

Of course, some families face more chronic, dysfunctional conflicts. This more severe brand of conflict will be covered in the next chapter.

Chapter Four

Blind Behavior

If first-degree conflict is about solving problems, and second-degree conflict is about power plays or psychological warfare, then third-degree conflict is all about dysfunctional behavior.

Some family problems never seem to get solved. Some kids in the family never grow up. Some other kids try mightily to grow up, but others in the family seem intent on stopping them. Trivial conflicts may drag on for years, while profoundly troubling issues get swept under the rug.

Instead of solving its problems, somehow the family is spinning its wheels, blaming or ignoring, but certainly not being effective. Common sense solutions can be seen in plain sight, yet most of the family can't get as far as noticing the problem, much less doing anything about it. ("Oh, don't worry, your Dad will stop drinking. It's nothing.")

This third-degree category finds people behaving so oddly it results in irony. Does Dad need to stop drinking? He'll think about it over his scotch. Does Mom need to stop nagging? She'll get to it as soon as you wipe your shoes, pick up your coat, and get that exasperated look off your face. And you, perhaps, might want to look at how it is that you plunge headfirst into craziness the moment you step inside your parents' house.

The essential problem is blind behavior. These chronic breakdowns aren't necessarily due to malice or spite, even though hostility may churn just below the surface. Instead, things are going so poorly because people have lost their ability to notice their own behavior. And no sooner do we arrive than we take our place in the dance.

"Watch me: I'll walk through that door and I'll become twelve years old again."

What happened? You were a successful adult: an investment banker, a carpenter, a student, or a parent. Perhaps you were a little nervous about seeing your folks, but you were still a functioning adult. Still the fine, solid citizen you'd worked so hard to become.

Then it all fell apart. One snide word from your brother, a dismissive glance from your dad, and there you were flailing like a twelve-year-old trying to play Rocky. What happened? That's your Volvo parked out front. Those are your kids playing video games. What happened to your common sense, and how did you get to be twelve years old again?

LEVEL THREE CONFLICT: BLIND BEHAVIOR

Conflict at Level Three has long outlived any purpose it might have ever had. These are strangely tireless conflicts. They defy common sense and will not end.

The following types of conflict all fall under the category of blind behavior:

- Draining family fights that continue to make people unhappy and never seem to go anywhere

- Any conflict where someone is stuck in the wrong decade

- Drug or alcohol abuse that hasn't yet escalated to physical harm or criminal behavior

- Any conflict involving long-standing prejudices around race, religion, or sexuality

- Codependence or the enabling of other destructive behavior

Examples of blind behavior might include:

- Your father criticizing every word that comes out of your mouth, as he has for years

- Your mother nagging you about getting your teeth fixed, and your refusing to do so

- A perennially unemployed but charming sibling, who has lived on hand-outs for years without trying to help himself

- Your sister being smarmy about your date because he's of a different ethnicity than you are

- A fierce sibling rivalry that might have made sense some decades ago, but is increasingly out of control

These examples may seem like an odd mix, with charming sorts mixed in with abrasive types. But charm isn't the issue: it's likely you've known some absolute snakes who knew how to be pleasant. At times, the key issue is self-awareness. If you lose the ability to see your problems, then you lose the ability to fix your mistakes. For instance:

- Does an alcoholic know she drinks too much? No.

- Does an overindulgent mother know that she "babies" grown children? No.

- Does a brutally critical father know he's being unreasonable? No.

- Can everyone else see that these are glaring problems? Well, pretty much everyone can, except for those who enable the same behaviors listed above.

A problem in someone's blind spot can grow and fester in a way that would never be tolerated under normal circumstances. *Blind spots* aren't a sign of bad character. Every car has a blind spot, and every human has one, too. However, when something falls into your blind spot, it can cause real damage.

Now, this chapter will not cover the profound damage resulting from predation or outright tyranny. That kind of conflict is so destructive that a separate chapter is needed to cover it adequately. (See chapter 5 for a more complete discussion.) Therefore, this chapter on blind behavior does not discuss the following:

- Physical abuse

- Theft, or embezzlement of family finances

- Alcohol, drug, or gambling abuse that results in violence, harm, or felonies

- Neglect to the point of endangering health or life (for example, blacking out while driving, and nearly totaling the car)

- Sexual abuse or incest

THE TROUBLE WITH BLIND BEHAVIOR

When people run into their blind spots they often get oddly stuck, fighting the same fights and repeating the same mistakes in an endless cycle. In the normal course of things, people bounce in and out of problem-solving. But by Level Three, people just dig themselves in deeper.

For instance, Betsy described her infuriating mother this way: "She won't listen, won't listen, won't listen. And then when she finally does hear me, she cries." Of course, then Betsy feels guilty and takes back everything she's said to her mother, and they're both right back where they started from. Despite anger, angst, and considerable hard work, nothing changes.

Here were intelligent people who sincerely wanted their lives to get better, who were willing to do the hard work, and who still weren't making any progress. The kept making the same mistakes.

Their therapists might have told them they weren't trying hard enough, but that wasn't necessarily true. Often they were trying very hard. They just weren't getting anywhere.

The key to the problem was that these people couldn't see their own behavior. They could describe in detail what was wrong with everyone else, but they couldn't spot their own mistakes, except for their puzzling lack of progress.

If they started a fight, they didn't know they had started it. They thought the other person had provoked it. If they broke a promise, they were convinced it was someone else's fault. The tenacious problems in their lives were all ascribed to other people, even if those people had been dead for twenty years.

Their own behavior was squarely located in their blind spot. Because they couldn't see their behavior, they couldn't change it, and so they repeated the same mistakes.

So, let's see how to make progress in the baffling range of blind behavior. We'll look at how to get better results from other people, as well as how you can do better yourself.

Normal Skills Fail

By this point on the Conflict Continuum, many of the usual skills of problems-solving fail. For instance, we normally solve problems by talking about them, but at this point, conversation doesn't work very well.

Let's say you speak with your sister who has a gambling problem. You might have a sensible discussion, even a breakthrough, filled with good points and common sense. Using all your persuasion skills and tact, you get her to see the light and agree to stop gambling. Then, the next morning, she goes off to the casino. The whole arrangement evaporates, leaving you wondering if you hallucinated the whole discussion.

Conversation and common sense have surprisingly little effect in this range. You might explain to your father that he doesn't need to criticize your job. But instead of hearing you, he insists that he's not criticizing and tells you that you have no sense of humor. Then he makes a really nasty wisecrack about your job—the same one he said he wasn't criticizing.

Stuck in Time

Another source of blind behavior is when families get stuck in the wrong decade.

I once accompanied an old friend to her childhood hometown, where most of her family still lived. This friend was a beautiful and successful professional, an accomplished writer, and a former model. Few people outside of Hollywood had as much going for her as she did.

During my visit, her older sister dropped by, and they took me on a tour of their neighborhood. I watched in amazement as my dazzling friend morphed into a scruffy kid trailing behind her older sister, stumbling and scuffing her shoes in the dirt. I remember checking the skies for cosmic rays. Nothing else could have explained the transformation.

Lost in time, we often behave in ways that make no sense. Laura and Alice were two sisters who had grown up with a father who hated phone calls. Once, when their dad was visiting Laura, she called her sister Alice. She whispered into the phone, "Alice, are you there?" Alice, whispering back, asked: "Laura, is this a secret phone call?" Her sister said, "Yes! Now listen . . ."

During Hurricane Katrina, this same Laura organized her friends to into a relief run to the devastated gulf region, trucking supplies into backcountry Louisiana where the Feds couldn't go. Yet when her dad came to visit, she was still concealing phone calls.

Your family may view you through the same kind of time-warp. They may be stuck on a "you" from the past, perhaps the sickly kid who was a bit of a dork. They think they're being kind by wrapping you up in a wool scarf, since you were always frail as a child. You feel annoyed because you just ran the Boston Marathon. Actually, they're acting appropriately, they're just in the wrong decade.

They can't understand that they've disrespected you because they don't see you in the here and now. If you snap at them, they'll look hurt and puzzled. It's not that you don't want them to care about you. You just want them to care for the you who actually exists today, not the one you've outlived.

Disrespect

Time-warp disrespect can happen no matter how successful you are. Mark, a prominent surgeon, once recalled how his parents had talked about a new pesticide they were considering for their lawn. Concerned, Mark researched the data and got back to them with a full report, only to discover that they'd already bought the stuff on the advice of the old guy who lived next door.

Mark fumed, "Who are they going to believe? Their own son with twelve years of graduate school, or a retired plumber? Of course they'll take the retired plumber because I'm their son and what would I know?"

It's one thing for your parents to lose track of time and treat you as if you were a child again, but it's another thing for you to "lose it" and revert to being a flailing teenager. It will be easier for you to calmly demand your due as an adult if you present yourself as unshakably grown.

EXERCISE: DO A REALITY CHECK

Now, for a moment, visualize your parents and siblings. How old are they now? What color is their hair? Are they taller than you or shorter? Chubby? Thin? Do they look powerful? Frail?

When you have their images clearly in mind, take out your journal or notebook, and then write brief descriptions of them.

The next time you see your family, pull out the descriptions you just wrote and see how they compare. They may not be very powerful anymore. Your vision of them may be as distorted as their vision of you.

Next, ask yourself: "How am I different from what my relatives expected me to be?" Write your answers to this question in your journal or notebook.

Next, ask yourself: "How did I come out similar to what they expected?" Then write down your answer to this question.

Then, ask yourself this question: "Do I like how I turned out?" Whether you like the way you turned out or you don't, write in your journal or notebook why you feel this way.

These kinds of reality checks will help to keep you grounded in the here and now, and they may keep you from getting bogged down in things that aren't true.

The Quicksand Effect

Level Three is home to the quicksand effect, where the harder you struggle, the faster you sink. For instance, the harder Mark, the surgeon, strove to be heard and taken seriously by his parents, the more he was disregarded. In this range, not only do the usual efforts not work, they may leave you worse off than you were before.

For example, Marge's father, a recent widower, had become romantically involved with a horrible, grasping woman. Marge tried to tell him that she thought his relationship wasn't such a good idea. In response, her father stopped taking her phone calls and asked the woman to marry him. In fact, the harder Marge worked to convince him that this woman was a mistake, the more he romanticized her behavior.

With the quicksand effect, your best efforts backfire. Like yelling at an alcoholic to stop drinking, the harder you argue, the less convincing you become.

Bill, a young man of twenty-four, worked at his family's restaurant business, where his mother was frequently rude to employees and customers alike. Bill found this mortifying. Finally he snapped at his mother to stop yelling at people.

Of course his mother didn't stop—she yelled louder. The more Bill yelled at her to be civil, the worse his mother yelled at the employees. Finally, Bill realized that he was just making things worse for everyone involved, so he gave up and left.

SOLUTION: DON'T FOLLOW THEM INTO QUICKSAND—INSIST THEY COME OUT OF IT

It sounds counterintuitive, but when you encounter the quicksand effect, you must resist the temptation to thrash heedlessly. Instead, behave as if you're facing actual quicksand: keep your head, move slowly and methodically, and pull people out rather than charging in yourself.

In Bill's story, it might have been better had he kept his voice low and steady, and perhaps talked to his mother away from the restaurant rather than surrounded by her usual triggers.

At Level Three, you often see a web of people stuck in blind behavior, with subtle ways of reinforcing the old, stuck patterns. Some of them will be more amenable to change than others. Work on the easiest ones first. They, in turn, can become your allies in getting the others to change.

In the case above, the mother was probably the most entrenched. Fine; talk to other influential ones first. Start with the sanest ones; ask their advice. Get them on board with your project. Then, when you're ready to approach the mother, she will be surrounded by people who are ready to see her change, rather than subtly provoking or enabling her worst.

Bullying and Increasing Overkill

Bullying appears at Level Three. After all, bullying is just a humiliating power play, done over and over. It's overkill and then some. It doesn't much matter if the bullying is verbal or physical, if the result is crushing the spirit of the other person.

Consider Zoe, a young woman who was visiting her parents in rural Pennsylvania. As a rule, Zoe didn't get along with her father, but the trip was going smoothly until they all went out to an Amish restaurant. The food was good and the portions were huge, with Dutch apple pie included in the meal.

Too full to eat her desert, Zoe had her pie boxed to go. She couldn't resist it completely, though, and as everyone else dug into dessert she cracked open the take-out box and broke off a piece of crust.

Her father went ballistic over this trivial act. "You'd think we'd raised an animal," he barked.

Zoe fought back, but then other diners began to stare. Then she swallowed her fury while her father continued berating her, privately feeling sorry for herself for having such an ignorant father.

Her dad continued ridiculing her clothes, her job, and her high-class education. Yet she was wearing nice clothes and had a good job. In fact, he was not only furious about what she had done wrong; it became clear he was even angrier about the things she'd done right.

SOLUTION: INCREASE YOUR RANGE OF MOTION

It's easy to bully children; they're small, know little about the world, and have only the resources their parents give them. Bullying adults, however, is an entirely different story. Adults have a free range of motion.

Zoe got caught up in meeting the sheer firepower of her father's attack. It didn't matter that he wasn't making sense and she had little to gain by joining in. She met the quicksand effect: the harder she struggled, the worse things got, until she gave up and did nothing. At least the fight ended, though it hardly felt good.

Instead, let's look at the situation while applying an adult range of motion.

You might start with the flood control techniques discussed in earlier chapters. If you can't think, you're essentially helpless, so start by breathing and clearing your head.

Next, assert some boundaries. Whatever the two of you need to discuss, it shouldn't be done at the top of your lungs in the middle of an Amish restaurant.

You might try talking your father down but, realistically, that may not work. Remember, conversations often fail around blind behavior. People are more deaf to input, more rigid, and more self-righteous. None of these is a component for a successful conversation.

So you can start with words to establish your boundaries, but if those don't work, explore your range of motion. For instance, in an Amish restaurant you might:

- Declare it's time to visit the bathroom and simply walk away.

- Leave and inspect the gift shop.

- Take your pie and wait outside.

- Visit the horses waiting with their buggies. You'll have better odds for finding a good conversation.

You can't be trapped now the way you were when you were a child. The cage has no walls anymore.

Believes Own Lies

With blind behavior, people believe their own lies. The father raging at his daughter over a piecrust fully believed she had disgraced the family. He believed all the insults he yelled at her. And if someone were to ask who had caused that scene, he would have insisted that his daughter Zoe did it, with her shocking manners.

Perspective doesn't work at Level Three. At this level, you may feel as though you've entered a reality-free zone.

It's disorienting when people sound so sincere as they say these untrue things. It can make you doubt your sanity. Here are some examples of lies told at Level Three, said with disorienting earnestness:

- "I can stop drinking anytime." (Said by an alcoholic.)

- "I worked hard to support you despite your worthless mother." (He was years behind in child support, and your mother was a lovely woman.)

- "I never lied to your father!" (She cheated on him for years.)

- "We're doing fine. This house has never looked so good." (There are gutters missing from the last storm, the upstairs bedroom has sprung a leak, and the garage has started to lean to one side.)

- "Your sister means the world to me." (Said as your lecherous brother-in-law maneuvers you into a corner.)

Because these lies are said with such heartfelt sincerity, you may wonder if you aren't imagining things, including, perhaps, the gutters or your brother-in-law's creeping hands. You feel torn between believing people who are supposed to love you and what you see with your own open eyes.

Part of what makes these lies so disorienting is that the usual signals of someone lying aren't necessarily present. We all lie sometimes, and we all have subtle cues that give things away when we're stretching the truth. However, when people believe their own lies, many of those cues aren't there. They may even sound convincing in a surreal kind of way.

Their justifications sound equally weird. The following statements are typical of someone who's been caught lying while engaged in blind behavior:

- "My memory really isn't very good."

- "Yeah, yeah, yeah. Start in on me again."

- "Why are you always dredging up the past?"

- "How would I know? I'm just your _____."

- "Why are you always picking on me?"

- "Don't you have anything better to do?"

Remember, conversations may not work well around blind behavior. So perhaps you need another plan.

SOLUTION: GO BY WHAT THEY DO, NOT BY WHAT THEY SAY

Rather than get confused by a raft of strange excuses, go by what they do, not by what they say.

Your brother-in-law may profess to be a loving husband, but he acts like a common lecher. Ignore his words, go by what he does. If his hand starts wandering at Thanksgiving dinner, feel free to jab it with a fork.

Your sister insists that she can stop drinking at any time, yet her problems have multiplied and she never quite manages to stay dry very long. Her words say she's fine but her actions say she's an alcoholic. Disregard her words and go by her actions. If you're close enough to rally the family, you might schedule an intervention. If you do, it will be one of the most challenging conversations of your life, so prepare ahead of time and get professional support.

It's fine to start with a conversation, but depend on actions. You can talk to your sister about her drinking, but participation in Alcoholics Anonymous or another formal recovery program are the things that are likely to work. You can warn your brother-in-law to knock it off, but brute force or exposure is more likely to succeed.

SOMETHING MUST BE WRONG WITH *YOU*

When people fall into blind behavior they don't doubt themselves. They feel surprisingly sure of themselves, especially considering how badly they're behaving. In fact, they're more likely to insist that something's wrong with *you*.

Josh was the younger of two sons raised by two alcoholics. His older brother, Mike, was the favorite, but they'd both had a rough time as children. Josh was aware his older brother had absorbed their parents' practice of denial, if not their drinking problem.

One day, Josh was talking with his brother, who casually mentioned that they had had good parents. This was a mind-numbing piece of denial that erased a good deal of their childhood.

Josh was dumbfounded. He'd managed to forgive their parents, but they had been appalling. He caught his breath and said, *"What?"* Mike blandly replied, "Well, my memory isn't all that good."

Josh began to flood, so he concentrated on that, rather than becoming incoherent with indignation. In fact, he was still working on controlling his flooding when his brother happened to mention basketball.

Now, the two brothers were quite competitive, and for years Mike had walloped Josh in pick-up basketball. Fresh from Mike's staggering denial about the their family, Josh cheerfully lied, "Yeah! Basketball—boy, I used to kick your butt! Remember—you could never beat me!" And then he proceeded to rewrite their childhood in a way that Josh preferred.

The curious part was Mike's reaction to this bald-faced lie. He just looked sheepish and allowed Josh to get away with it. Mike didn't admit he had been busted, but he looked and acted busted. And whether or not Mike changed, Josh got a great laugh out of this conversation and genuinely felt better. Even more curious, during the next several conversations Mike made no further attempts to rewrite their past.

Josh found he didn't need to fight to the end to prove his brother had discounted their reality, or to rub his brother's nose in their parents' failings. What Josh wanted was to not feel crazy.

Highly Charming or Manipulative

Parents are apt to pull out the stops when they want more attention from their children. For example, a number of people have reported that their elderly parents will sometimes call up, feign a crisis, get their kids to drive over in a panic, and then blithely admit that the crisis was a scam. They make no apology, just sit the kids down for coffee. It's as if all's fair in love, war, and getting the kids to come over.

Louis's mother was less charming and more manipulative. He used to visit his mother regularly, but she had learned that if she wanted him to stay longer, all she had to do was bring up Louis's ex-wife. That would spark a fight, which would gain her more attention.

Louis had told her dozens of times that he did not want to discuss his ex any more, which only made it more infuriating when his mom kept doing it anyway.

Since his mother kept pulling the same trick, Louis knew precisely how to prepare. The next time his mother brought up his ex-wife as he prepared to leave, he didn't flood. He picked up a box of books he was planning to take with him and said, "Bye, Mom." His mother followed him to the door, still chattering about the ex-wife. Louis hefted the box of books a few times to control his flooding and repeated, "Bye, Mom," and kept walking.

Not used to this, his mother started flooding, which had never happened before. Louis, surprised that his mother was stammering while he wasn't, just kept picking up more boxes and repeating, "Bye, Mom."

SOLUTION: ACT IN YOUR OWN INTEREST

When putting up with blind behavior, there's a curious tendency to passively accept the unacceptable. This holds true even when acting in your own interest would be as simple as saying, "Bye." Feeling outwitted or somehow outgunned, we don't react at all. We put up with tantrums we would never accept from other human beings, or insults we'd never consider listening to. We have no idea how to react and, so, we do nothing at all.

It feels strangely natural when family members overrun boundaries, even as we're shocked that they try. Perhaps it's their job to try it; but if that is the case, perhaps it's our job to stop it. We can always pick up the conversation later, over the phone perhaps.

Be realistic. If you don't set boundaries, there aren't going to be any. Be fair and be polite, but decide on your limits ahead of time and then follow up with action.

Escaping Blind Behavior

By far, the lion's share of the behavior I've been discussing is performed by parents and relatives acting out. Obviously, it's parents who become stubborn, rigid, and unreasonable, who ignite fights and refuse to admit they're ever wrong. And although we might have grown up in the same house and learned the bulk of our behaviors there, we would never do such a thing.

Right?

Wrong. The reality is that these behaviors have a powerful gravitational pull. Power plays meet with opposing power plays—sometimes with furious defiance, and sometimes with sullen resistance and self-pity, but with an answering power play just the same. Rudeness breeds rudeness. Yelling breeds yelling. It's the family way. Two can play at this game and do, often.

Two, however, will not end the cycle. Only one person will be able to lead the way out; that one has got to be you. You will have to take the lead here, because nothing is going to happen if you leave it to your family members.

This may strike you as utterly unjust. Why should you have to change? They've been tormenting you for years! They're wrong—they should change! That's what's just.

But justice has nothing to do with this. If the world operated on the basis of justice, there would be fewer people and many more piles of smoldering ash where a deserving soul was just struck by lightening. By now, I hope, you've given up expecting your relatives to spontaneously combust, no matter how deeply they deserve it. Since they're still around, and you're still around, it's for you to take the situation in hand.

You're an adult now, and it's your job to run your world better than any of those who handed the world to you.

I'd like to present you with a quick and easy fix; instead, I'm going to offer you a hard one: Do not attempt to change the other person. Change yourself.

If you are embroiled with another person—say, one who practices blind behavior—you will end up displaying related behaviors that are every bit as disturbing as that other person's. It's like the addict and the codependent, the control freak and the enabler, the oppressor and the victim. Where you find one you find the other. Like salt and pepper, it's a matched set.

You have got to get out of this mess, but first, you'll need to regain control over your own behavior. You'll need to step out of your own blind spot.

You may object again: "But they're the ones who screwed me up!"

I won't dispute that. But if they're the ones who did so much damage, it's surely foolish of you to think they're now going to fix it. If they had that kind of wisdom, they wouldn't have damaged you in the first place.

You may object that they're the ones with the drinking problem, the chronic unemployment, the endless parade of broken marriages. It's not your fault.

I'm sure it isn't, but that's irrelevant. The fair thing might be to get them to do the work, but life isn't fair and they're not about to do the work. They didn't find this book. You did. And, if you do the work, you get the payoff. That's a different kind of fairness.

OVERVIEW OF BLIND BEHAVIOR

Here is an overview of the issues that come up in the dysfunctional world of blind behavior:

- Conflict stuck in a downward spiral

- Conflict feels like quicksand

- Loss of perspective

- Missing boundaries

- Believes own lies

- Highly charming or manipulative

These patterns are generally found around:

- Chronic, draining conflicts

- Conflicts stuck in the past

- Early-stage addictions

- Bias or prejudice of all sorts

At this level, many of the usual skills, like common sense or conversation, don't work well. Instead, we'll have to look at other solutions. Note that the third section of the book (chapters 6 through 9) will cover more skills yet.

SOLUTIONS FOR BLIND BEHAVIOR

Here are some ways to handle the problems that arise from blind behavior.

Problem

Your father routinely belittles you and bullies you in public. It's automatic. He doesn't even think about it anymore.

Solutions

Watch what they do, not what they say. He says it's just a joke, yet you've repeatedly told him how much it bothers you. Don't doubt your feelings. Humor that causes pain is hostility, not fun.

Stay in the here and now. Take a close look at this old guy who's giving you such a hard time. Is he ridiculing your looks because you have a full head of hair and he doesn't?

Don't go into the quicksand. Make them come out. Don't get drawn into complaints that you are oversensitive. Insist he treat you like a fellow adult. If he can't, go away until he can.

Restore perspective. Act accordingly. Secure people don't bully. Insecure people do. Ask yourself: "Is all this because I have more hair than you do?" You don't have to say it aloud. Just thinking it clearly can change that particular conversation forever.

Problem

Your brother-in-law keeps putting the moves on you.

Solutions

Watch what they do, not what they say. He says he adores your sister, then reaches for you.

Stay in the here and now. You're an adult and you don't have to take this from anyone.

Restore perspective. Act accordingly. The problem is his behavior, not yours. Publicly embarrass him. Don't let him privately embarrass you.

Don't go into the quicksand. Make them come out.   If your sister wants to blame you, don't get embroiled. Let her deal with her husband. This has nothing to do with you.

Problem

Your mom overdramatizes things. Always has.

Solutions

Watch what they do, not what they say.   She complains, then does nothing. She seems to forget the whole thing after a while. In fact, she seems to be in her comfort zone.

Restore perspective. Act accordingly.   Listen in a kindly way, but disconnect from her agitation. It's not doing you any good and it isn't doing her any good, either.

Stay in the here and now.   You're speaking to a grown woman who has handled many problems in her long life. Surely she's seen worse. Talk with her about that, grown-up to grown-up.

Don't go into the quicksand. Make them come out.   Don't join in her drama. If she's interested, let her join your calm. Besides, there's no sign anything's actually wrong.

EXERCISE: HANDLING EVERYDAY CASES OF BLIND BEHAVIOR

Now you try it. Think of a chronic, bewildering conflict in your family where people exhibit some or all of the symptoms of blind behavior. Problems would include:

- People blind to their own behavior

- Relatives behaving as if you were in the wrong decade

- People who believe their own lies

- Bullying

- Rage seizures (but not going as far as physical violence)

- The quicksand effect

- Nearly anything concerning an addiction (although again not going as far as physical harm)

In the past, you might have exhibited the following behaviors:

- Inability to act in your own interest

- Believing openly unbelievable lies

- Losing your perspective

- Reacting with overkill

Now, think of a conflict where some or all of these factors came into play. Describe it in your journal or separate notebook.

Think of how you might operate in terms of what they do rather than what they say. (*Example:* Your charming, irresponsible brother has repeatedly borrowed, then damaged, your power tools. Each time he promises to do better. The last one cost you $200.)

In your journal or notebook, make two lists: One list should say, "What They Say" and the other, "What They Do." Your lists should look like this:

What They Say   **What They Do**

_____   _____

_____   _____

_____   _____

_____   _____

Now picture this relative in the here and now. See yourself as an adult, with all the choices of an adult. You have money in your pocket and your own set of car keys. So does he. Neither one of you is helpless.

What options do you have now that perhaps you didn't have as a child? If he's too dependent on you, think of his own choices. In the case of the broken power tools, for example, your brother can replace the loaners he's broken, or he can find a different source for tools that doesn't involve you.

Write down your options in your journal or notebook.

Now it's time to rethink your approach. Considering what these relatives do against what they say, base your decision only on what they actually do. Keep in mind that you're both fully grown. (In the case of the broken tools, you might decline to loan him your good power tools. You might give him extra tools you no longer want, or you might suggest a company where he can rent or buy the tools he needs.)

Write down your solution in your journal or notebook.

Now think of how you might keep from becoming embroiled in the family quicksand. For instance, if your brother complains to your mother that you're being unfair, politely hand him the Yellow Pages and then go through the refrigerator and make yourself a sandwich. (Staying out of quicksand is hungry work.) You might make a sandwich for your brother as well, but keep him away from your power tools.

Write down your own plan in your journal or notebook.

Now if this or a similar situation comes up again, you have a series of different solutions you might try.

Some families take all of these dysfunctions and add violence or sexual assault to create a witch's brew of awful dynamics. Those families are discussed in the next chapter.

Chapter Five

Predation or Tyranny

By Level Four, the rules of conflict change again. By the time people have become tyrants or predators they aren't just blind to their own behavior, they are so out of control they've become a danger to themselves and others in the family.

Your family may not have problems this severe. In that case, you may wish to simply skip this chapter. However, problems like late-stage addictions have become so common that they might appear in a family you marry into, or the family of a close friend. In that case, you may want to become familiar with these issues, because they will have an effect on those you love.

Tyrannical or predatory behavior includes all of the profoundly destructive family traumas. These include:

1. Domestic violence

2. Child abuse

3. Sexual abuse

4. Late-stage addictions

5. Extreme personality disorders, such as psychopathology

6. Theft or embezzling from the family

Now you may feel that theft or embezzlement is relatively benign compared to the other abuses listed. However, stealing from your own family is such a marked betrayal that it's usually caused by one of the other disorders—say, a drug addict stealing her mother's jewelry to feed her habit.

You may also feel uneasy thinking of your sweet Uncle Charlie as a tyrant when he's merely a constant drunk who's destroying his liver. Uncle Charlie isn't the tyrant; alcohol is. Charlie hasn't been in charge in years. Left unchecked, the alcohol will kill Charlie and destroy his family in the process. Charlie may be very nice; but the drug he depends on isn't, and the drug is the threat to the family.

Extreme personality disorders can also create a predator, even if violence is never involved. A psychopath may be outwardly charming and never lift a hand against her kin; the damage she inflicts is purely emotional. In a similar vein, someone with a destructive narcissistic pattern is so extraordinarily needy and self-absorbed that he will sacrifice his kids to his insatiable ego.

Such a person may commit no specific crimes; the disorder is more like emotional cannibalism. As one survivor put it, "My mother didn't want to kill me, she just tried to suck out my bone marrow." So it is possible to live under Level Four predation without physical scars to show for it. However, it definitely will leave scars of some sort.

Tyrants or predators also operate in their blind spots, as in Level Three. Ask a late-stage addict if she has a problem and she'll insist in all sincerity that she doesn't. Physically violent abusers will earnestly claim they're fine, but that others provoked them. Perhaps it was wrong to break Jimmy's arm, but the predator will insist he really had no choice.

Apart from the difference in severity in this category, there are differences in the damage done and in which techniques will be most effective. Level Three dysfunction can certainly cause problems and earn you a few years in therapy. Level Four tyranny, however, does profound and lasting harm. Level Three blind behavior is an exasperating part of human nature, part of the flawed world we live in. Level Four predation can't be lived with safely. It's simply too destructive.

FELONIES

All families have their moments but, by this point, they're having moments that could put those they love in the hospital. Under tyranny, rage seizures have muscle behind them. It's damaging enough to lose control verbally. To lose control while physically trying to hurt members of your own family is terrifying and not entirely normal.

Examples of felony-level rage seizures include:

1. Striking people with full force

2. Destroying objects as a show of power

3. Destroying furniture

4. Threatening harm

5. Threatening with weapons

6. Using weapons, whether or not they miss

Slamming down books on a table is a show of temper. It's loud, but hurts no one. Smashing someone's beloved china collection in a sustained fury is a rage seizure.

Kids might get into knock-down fights as part of growing up. A three-year-old may completely abandon herself in a raging tantrum. The house will survive and the adults will be annoyed but unhurt. It's altogether different when adults lose control to the point where they hardly know what they're doing.

If you talk to such people later, they may not always remember what they've done. A rage seizure can be the rough equivalent of an alcoholic blackout, which means that while they were destroying the place, there was no one in control.

Sometimes, after such a blackout, some abusers may maintain a façade of being in charge. They may insist it was someone else's fault, then order others in the family to clean up the mess. Meanwhile their eyes dart around, secretly assessing just what it is they wrecked.

The familiar skills of accusation, manipulation, and whining are still in play, even when physical damage is done. Here are some examples of statements that abusers make to excuse themselves from responsibility:

1. "See what you've made me do!"

2. "You know I don't want to be this way. Why do you push me like that?"

3. "Can't you see what you're doing here?!"

4. "I hope you're happy now."

That strange lack of self-awareness is still in play, along with the disorienting ability to believe their own lies.

Solution: Let Them Carry Their Own Weight

Glowering, terrifying, forceful abusers are actually quite needy. You can hear it in their whining and manipulating to be forgiven or admired. You can even see it in the swaggering bullying: they need someone to feel superior to, to blame for all their troubles.

The tyrant may need you, but not in a healthy manner. The thief needs someone to steal from. The abuser needs someone to frighten. The sexual predator needs someone to molest. The victim doesn't need any of this. The predator is the one who's so needy.

Codependents pick up on the neediness and latch onto it in an unfortunate way. They tell themselves this neediness is a form of love, even a form of honor. That's just not true. Someone who's loved can cut a much better deal than getting yelled at and slapped around once a month.

Tyrants may need you to hurt or humiliate or to sexually compromise. They might need you to tolerate the intolerable. You, however, do not need them. So think of how you might withdraw your cooperation.

Some examples of withdrawing cooperation might include:

1. Your sister, on drugs, threatens you and expects you to cringe or capitulate. Instead you call the police and press charges.

2. Your uncle, who was always creepy, tries putting the moves on you and expects you to lie to the family. You don't.

3. Your brother steals from the family company and expects you to cover for him. Instead you turn the books over to the accountant.

EXERCISE: EXAMINE WITH FRESH EYES

Just for a moment, picture the predator in your life. Do some flood control if you need it. Think of the tyrant doing her usual crime, and knowing that you know. How would she expect you to accommodate her or cover for her? Some typical examples might be to avert your eyes to abuse, pretend you don't hear, or abet her in some way, such as fudging a time card or helping her fill a prescription that you know isn't legal.

Now, in your journal or notebook, write down how she might expect you to play along.

After you've finished writing, think of something different you might do, that would not cater to this unhealthy need. For instance, you might call your lecherous uncle's wife into the room, decline to sign a forged time card, or simply leave the prescription on the table.

Just to experiment, think of some unexpected things you might do. You don't have to be dramatic or commit yourself to doing these things. Just consider actions that would be outside your usual pattern.

Write down those possible actions in your journal or notebook.

Right now, the abuser has a worldview where he or she is in control and you are just a puppet. This mind-set wasn't created to do you any good. In order to move toward health and freedom, you will have to cut the strings to the puppeteer. The rest of this chapter will provide you with a variety of ways to do that.

COLLAPSE OF BOUNDARIES

By this point in the continuum, normal standards have collapsed. The social contract is broken. Normal people can't go on like this, and they can't stay normal in the midst of it.

Youngsters exposed to this kind of behavior grow up unsure of what normal behavior might be, or how families are supposed to behave. Kids who witness abuse often have an intuitive sense that the abuse they see can't possibly be right. Still, since the adults around them act as if abuse is normal, children learn to doubt their own instincts. They come away puzzled by how normal behavior might work.

As behavior deteriorates, the family can't function. One of the hallmarks of Level Four conflict is that life becomes so unmanageable that the family needs outside professionals to step in just to get through life. Outsiders may include:

1. Cops

2. Doctors

3. Social workers

4. Addiction counselors

5. Lawyers

6. Parole officers

If any of these people visited your family when you were growing up—or you wished they had—you may have grown up in the midst of predatory behavior. These outsiders keep getting called in because behavior has become so distorted that the family can't be relied on to solve its own problems. The family is out of control. A perfect stranger is needed to set things straight.

In fact, many professions are largely devoted to repairing damage done at Level Four. For instance, psychologists rather rarely repair trauma resulting from a car wreck or an act of nature. Instead, much of their work involves repairing damage from family abuse, sexual abuse, or some deliberate human act.

Solution: Trust a Pro

Growing up around predators or tyrants may leave you with a profound distrust of others, particularly helping or authority figures. That's reasonable; the powerful figures in your life were probably a lot of trouble. They were the last ones you could expect to count on.

However, all professionals don't merit your distrust. Some may be quite helpful. Don't trust just anyone, of course. Ask around among people you respect. Get some good referrals. For instance, Al-Anon meetings all follow the same format, but some meetings will suit you more than others. That's fine. Shop around, and see where you might best invest your trust.

Reasonable trust is a skill you'll want to learn. There's nothing wrong with practicing it in a safe venue, around professionals.

OTHERS LIE FOR THEM

Family predators don't keep their own secrets. They expect others to keep secrets for them. It's another example of their odd neediness. Strangely, they often get what they ask for. Usually, there's an element of threat implied in keeping their secrets. These include:

1. Overt threat: "If you ever tell, I'll get you."

2. Threat to loved one: "If anyone finds out, it would kill your mother."

3. Gaslighting: "No one will ever believe you."

4. Complicity: "If they find out you let this happen, they'll take the baby."

5. Hostage-taking: "If you ever tell, I'll make sure you lose the baby."

6. Implied threat: It remains unspoken yet somehow clear that something horrible will happen if the truth comes out.

Under duress, the secret becomes your own.

This turns into a form of hostage-taking. For instance, you may be aware that your cousin is funneling money from the family company. You know if this ever comes to light, the company as a whole might go under. The company is taken hostage to ensure your silence.

You don't keep the secret to protect your cousin, whom you may resent deeply. You do it to protect the rest of your family.

Solution: Tell One Person, and Choose Well

You may not be prepared to tell the world just what has been going on in your family, but you need to break the secret's hold over you. Once the secret morphs into a common fact, it will start to lose its power. Let the predator worry about secrets. It's for you to concentrate on the truth.

Telling secrets releases great power. Counselors who work with torture survivors relate that one of the paths to healing involves having these people tell their stories and be heard.

You need tell only one person to start to break the secret's hold, but choose that person well. A trustworthy counselor could be an excellent choice, because he or she has been down this road with other clients and can give you professional-strength support and advice about what your next step might be. Listen to that person about whether or not it's wise to discuss the problem with your family. Your family, after all, may not react well. A good counselor will help you work out your options.

Perhaps one of the most disturbing things about telling family secrets is to find out that everyone else already knows. All this time they may have kept silent for the same reasons that silenced you. They may have kept silent thinking they were protecting you.

You need to talk. You also need to find out just how far the damage goes. An excellent guide for this kind of work is the book by John Bradshaw, *Family Secrets: What You Don't Know Can Hurt You* (1995).

THE BELL JAR EFFECT

Family abuse routinely happens within a peculiar circle of silence, which I call the "bell jar effect." It's like being inside an isolating glass jar. The rest of the world is just a few feet away, and yet whoever is trapped in the bell jar can't reach out for help. They feel strangely alone. Molested children go to school and never say a word to anyone. You may know your sister is spiriting away family heirlooms, yet you don't say a word.

Whenever you see this phenomenon take shape, you must break the bell jar. The circle of silence can be imposed on children because they don't know what it is or what to do. The bell jar effect also happens to adults. However, you're older and you have different choices.

Ashley had grown up in a large family, often playing with a group of cousins. There was something wrong about some of these cousins, and the way they'd deliberately hurt others when they played. Still, they were family, and when many years later one of these cousins, Eric, traveled to her city, she didn't think twice about letting him sleep in her living room.

Once he arrived, however, she had a creepy feeling about him and locked her bedroom door that night. At 2 A.M. she heard him stealthily working at her door, trying to get in.

She had roommates throughout the house, and yet she said nothing about this until after he left the next day. Lying awake in silence, listening to him working at her door, was the bell jar effect in action. The solution was to shatter it. To shout, "Eric, go away," and flip the light switch on.

However, Ashley did speak of this to her family, since Eric would be around for the holidays and she had younger sisters. Her parents did and said nothing. Appalled, but somehow not surprised, she then spoke to her sisters herself. The sisters still kept his secret, but they took their own precautions.

The only way to fathom why this family would behave this way is to consider the unspoken threats. Ashley kept quiet about Eric essentially because she was afraid of him. Certainly she was afraid that he would be believed and she wouldn't. Her parents kept his secret from a vague, unspoken fear of how Eric's parents might retaliate.

Instead of doing anything effective they all ended up wishing the problem would somehow just go away. That isn't an effective plan of action.

Eric didn't wish for want he wanted; he acted. That left him the lone moving force in a landscape of denial.

Solution: Break the Bell Jar

Silence keeps you isolated and cut off from help. Instead, break the bell jar. Cross the distance and reach out for help.

You might choose to talk things over with any of the following:

1. A counselor

2. A support group

3. A lawyer

4. Trusted friends

5. The police

You want to chose a confidante who will help and not complicate things. If the incident happened long ago, choose someone who will:

1. Listen without judging you

2.   Believe you

3.   Show good judgment

4.   Be supportive of your decision, but not push you one way or
     the other

5.   Be discreet with whatever you tell him or her

In short, this person's role is to be a sounding board but not to
tell you what to do. You will retain the final decision in how you will
act. If the incident just happened—say, your drunken brother tried to
run you over with his car—then pick up the phone and call the police.
It's time to stop covering for these people.

LEARNED HELPLESSNESS

One of the most puzzling things about Level Four is that victims or
survivors don't act when they can. It becomes easier to understand this
in the light of a brutal experiment that taught dogs *learned helplessness*.

Dogs were placed in cages where they were trapped and given
electric shocks. When the voltage was turned on, at first the dogs
would struggle. But when that didn't work—when they couldn't escape
the shock—the dogs stopped struggling. They knew they couldn't get
away from it, so they gave up and did nothing.

Later, when the dogs had an easy way to avoid the shocks, they
still did not escape. They had learned the lesson of helplessness so
thoroughly that they wouldn't take even simple actions to save
themselves.

An experimenter was asked if there was ever a way to unlearn
learned helplessness. Evidently, at first, it was hard to teach these
profoundly sabotaged dogs to save themselves. The experimenters had
to reach into the cages and physically haul the dogs away from the
electric shock. They had to do this repeatedly, but after a while the
dogs got it, and then they would leap to save themselves. If, after that,
the experimenters tried again to teach the dogs to be helpless, it was
much harder to get the dogs to give up (Seligman 1992).

That was a harsh experiment, but similar training programs are
played out in abusive families all over the world. Children cannot
escape family tormentors. They don't have the skills, and have no

place to go. Nonetheless, what may have been done to you as a child cannot be done to you as an adult. You will never be as trapped again. But until you learn to save yourself when there is opportunity, you will be trapped in learned helplessness.

This is also why, as adults, we need to intervene if a child in the family is being abused. Long ago we learned to do nothing around Uncle Harry, and Uncle Harry outwitted us at every turn. Adults can do that to children. It's much, much harder for adults to do that to other adults.

The other fact to keep in mind is that abuse rarely happens only once. You may think Uncle Harry is over this kind of behavior because it stopped around you. Realistically, that may mean only that you outgrew the abuser's level of confidence. Other children now may be just as vulnerable as you were years ago.

JEKYLL AND HYDE BEHAVIOR

In the last case discussed, Eric came from a respectable family, which is not unexpected. Many predators maintain a handsome façade; they wouldn't be able to get away with nearly as much if they showed their true self to the world.

Predators often function as two entirely different people: a model citizen to the outside world, and a monster at home. This is part of the reason that victims don't talk. For them it really does feel like no one else would ever believe them.

For leading a double life, self-righteousness is a useful skill. Self-righteousness first appeared back at Level Two on the Conflict Continuum Chart. By Level Four it's a justification for unconscionable behavior. Self-righteousness isn't really about morality; it's a means for control and domination.

It's time to take a new look at self-righteousness. It isn't an emotion as much as it's a tool. Self-righteousness functions as a shield against unpleasant facts, reason, even, perhaps, a legal indictment.

Religious extremism or cults can use Jekyll and Hyde behavior to create a world of absolute control surrounded by a circle of silence. The self-righteous mask enables tyrants to feel superior while justifying whatever damage they do to others.

In her 2004 memoir, *Fierce*, Barbara Robinette Moss writes how she married a man as destructive as her father, although her husband was a fundamentalist and her father was an alcoholic. She describes her husband as having "such a special relationship with God that he was exempt from the strict code of moral behavior he imposed on the rest of us." He was one man in church, and quite someone else with his family. Moss didn't feel sanctified for having had this experience, but rather desperately diminished and nearly extinguished.

You can start by not believing the mask yourself. Think of the skills you learned in the last chapter: "Don't go by what they say but what they do." Predators and tyrants may portray themselves as righteous and beyond question, but if they act abusively, you must treat them as dangerous, not as someone acting for the divine.

Ongoing abuse is not about your sins or your supposed failings. If God wished to punish you, He wouldn't have sent your drunken uncle. The god that gets invoked is as strangely two-sided as the tyrant: supposedly gentle and loving, but also vicious and vindictive. This kind of behavior is not the sign of someone following a religious path. Rather, these are tyrants remaking the Divine in their own image: small, petty, and vindictive.

You do not need to submit to such a person. You need to keep him or her away from you.

Solution: The Wall and the Circle

Homes are built with four walls and a door, designed to keep danger outside. Storms and thieves are outside, while family and friends are inside. However, sometimes that system goes wrong, and a predator ends up inside the home instead of outside.

It may be Uncle Harry, who's a little "funny" around little girls. It may be Dad, who's put Mom in the hospital twice so far.

A family will unite against a foreign predator outside its walls; but if the tiger is inside the family circle, then the family doesn't call it a tiger, they call it "Grandpa," or "Aunt Sue." Often, the family will unite to protect the predator, insist there is no problem, and little Jimmy "just fell down some stairs."

Since boundaries in Level Four are terribly flawed, you need to create new ones. You need to redraw the family circle and move the danger back to the outside.

Let's say the predator in your family is a rageaholic. Anything can trigger her—a TV show, an unexpected word, the phase of the moon—and she starts spewing venom. You don't talk back or argue with her when she gets this way, because you have before and it's never worked.

Instead, gather up those you love and take them somewhere else. Put a protective circle around them and leave the raging terror outside of it. Take them all to the movies, or for a drive, or a walk around the neighborhood. Get them out of there.

Predators who are close family members may have trusted access to the family's bank accounts. They're inside the wall instead of outside. If they abuse the trust and steal from the family, move the circle. Change the authorization signatures on the accounts.

It was noted back at Level Three that victims stop acting in their own interest. You don't have to appease the thief, soothe the rageaholic, sober up the drunk, or enlighten the tyrant. Your job is not to change them; they're adults and can change themselves. Your job is to protect yourself and those who depend on you.

ADDICTIONS

If addictions are involved, there's a somewhat different line to be drawn. If a drug is the predator, it also has to be kept outside the wall, but you can distinguish between the drug and your relative. Aunt Josie may be fine when she's sober; Aunt Josie on meth is not. Aunt Josie is welcome inside the wall, but she can't take her friend meth in with her. Meth—the enemy—must stay outside.

Minimize Risk

Protection is the byword. Even though you may show patience toward Aunt Josie, never leave children alone with anyone with an addiction of any sort, whether early or late stage. That includes alcohol, drugs, and even gambling.

An early-stage addict may not yet be a danger to others, but you can't run the risk with your kids. The truth is, you have no way of knowing how far the addiction has gone. You may think your sister with the drinking problem can stay away from her gin for an afternoon, and so you leave your kids with her. But then she decides she needs a quick one—which becomes several. You come back to find your children taking care of her, since she got drunk and fell down the stairs.

You won't find out if your relative has lost control until something happens or your kids mention it to you, and that's really too late. Err on the side of caution. It's one thing for you, the adult, to run that kind of risk, but it's not alright to put your kids in that kind of situation.

Handling addicted family members is complicated by loyalty and the desperate desire to wish it all away. Amy Dickinson writes a gutsy advice column, where she once fielded a letter from a dad whose drunken father-in-law had made lewd gestures toward the man's infant son. The dad's wife wanted to forget the whole thing. Dad wasn't sure what to do.

Dickinson offered a succinct guideline. She said that the most sober person who is not in denial gets to decide what to do. Her advice was to protect the child and seal the wall. The father-in-law was not to be allowed around children while he was drinking, ever, and not be allowed to be alone with them unless he had proven himself safe beyond question (Dickinson 2005).

You don't have to make excuses to the father-in-law, turn yourself inside out to explain this in a way he can comprehend, or protect his feelings from the truth. You only need to keep the kids away from him.

The first step in controlling a tyrant or predator is to make them do their own work. They lie well enough for themselves. It's not your job to lie for them.

Hoffman's Rules

Dr. Virginia Hoffman teaches a course called "Christian Marriage" at Loyola University. As a formerly battered wife she formulated a list of guidelines for handling physical and emotional abuse. These are her suggestions for handling abusive or addictive situations:

1. *Name the problem,* at least in your own head. No more denial. This means you may be afraid to speak the truth to someone who is threatening you, but you need to speak the truth to yourself. Denial will not get you out of this. The truth can.

2. *Detach.* Don't let a predator or tyrant's behavior set your mood or your behavior. The abuser has quite enough power as it is. You need to regain control over your own spirit.

3. *Don't enable.* Don't make excuses, cover up, or come to the predator's rescue. Lying is the job of the predators. Make them do their own work.

4. *Set boundaries.* "I love you, but I won't stand here while you talk to me that way." Do not allow abuse to children—take them to a safe place or call 911. Don't ignore it if children are being abused; they cannot set boundaries effectively with adults. You need to erect a protective wall around yourself and the children. Children will not be able to build an effective wall against a predator. That's a job for adults.

5. *Get help for yourself.* Either Al-Anon or private counseling will do. This is a multilayered, formidable problem. It's not reasonable to think you can handle it alone. Al-Anon is free. Good therapy is more expensive, but worth it. You can pay for help now or pay for it later in damage and misery, but paying for it now is cheaper.

6. *Get a life.* Work on your own goals, do healthy things with friends or other family members. Get involved in positive activities. The predator will seek to be the center of your life. You need a healthy center that will serve you, not the tyrant.

7. *Find a place of peace within yourself.* You will need a stable core to see you through this hard time. Your home may change, your conditions may change, but you will always be with yourself. If you have a place of peace within yourself, it will always stay with you.

PROTECTION

If your family includes a predator, you may decide to keep your distance from your family as the best way to protect yourself and your loved ones. Staying away can be a responsible course of action, and may be less emotionally draining than even limited contact.

However, there may be times when you do need to have contact with them. All the family may not be equally damaging, and there may be emotional or even legal reasons why you need to deal with the others. In that case, you want to work out a plan ahead of time so that you can go into the situation and come out again unscathed.

At best, the terrain will be like quicksand, so don't go in and linger. Like a pleasant mood around a rageholic, peace could give way at any moment. Go in, do what you need to do, and then return to your own life. It may be wiser to invite your family to your home, one or two at a time, and deal with them in your world, rather than for you to go in to theirs.

If you do visit your family, make a concerted effort to listen to your instincts and act accordingly. This may prove surprisingly difficult.

After having lived through a profoundly crazy-making situation, you may have difficulty listening to your instincts. You may have been lied to and deceived in so many ways, your instincts may be thoroughly bewildered. You may have little faith in your own survival instincts, since they didn't protect you well in the past.

This means you have a new skill to acquire: Listen to your gut.

If you are in the presence of someone you don't trust, your body will try to get your attention. It may be queasiness in the pit of your stomach, or a sudden muscle twitch. Your shoulders may start to hurt or your back may go into spasm. Whatever it is, your body is trying to speak to you. It's now your job to listen.

Your body may not seem to make sense at first. For example, your shoulders may ache around everyone from your father's family, when it's only your father's uncle you've learned to dread. That's okay. It's alright to err on the side of caution. Later on, you may calm down around that side of the family, or you may discover what it is that disturbs you. For now, your job is simply to listen to your body, and do what you need to restore a feeling of safety.

Solution: Protect the Right Person

If you've lived through family abuse, you've probably become a fairly protective person. The problem is that most likely you learned to protect the predator rather than yourself.

A reader wrote to Dear Abby, saying that her mother-in-law was so oblivious that she had allowed her children to be physically and sexually abused by family members. These abusers were still present. The mother-in-law now wanted to keep her grandchildren overnight, so what should the parents say? Abby suggested that they should calmly inform the mother-in-law that she wouldn't be babysitting. If asked why, the children's mother should simply tell the truth. Protecting the young ones is more important than maintaining the mother-in-law's fantasy that all is well (Van Buren 2005).

Protection is a wonderful thing, but it should go to those who need it. A predator needs to face him- or herself, not be protected from their own behavior.

Predators are strangely adept at inspiring pity in others. It may pain you greatly that Grandpa took too great an interest in your bath. He may seem like a fragile old man now. If you really feel sorry for him, send him a nice card, but keep your children away from him.

It's one thing that you as a child trusted a predator. It's something else for you to be an easy mark now. Kindness, forgiveness, or religious faith have nothing to do with it. If your religion demands that you forgive them, fine; but that's different from sending your kids on a camping trip with them. Forgiveness is not code for stupidity. Your job is to act in the interests of your children.

You may think this relative is old now and no longer able to do any harm. Think again. It may be that you're too old for them to threaten. Predators are often afraid to approach adults. You may have outgrown the danger. Your kids haven't.

CREATING AN ACTION PLAN

Here is a list of different strategies for protecting yourself and your loved ones when a predator's in the family:

1. Move the circle, build a wall.

2. Protect any children.

3. Protect yourself.

4. Do not lie for a predator. Make him or her do their own work.

5. Shift the consequences back to the wrongdoer.

6. Refuse to keep a predator's secrets.

7. Get advice from someone with an outside perspective.

8. Beware of repeating the same pattern.

9. Break the bell jar.

10. Act in your own interest.

Examples for Handling Predation or Tyranny

Here are some different ways to deal with tyranny or predation in the family.

Problem

Your mom drinks and drives. She wants the kids this weekend.

Seek Help—Al-Anon is the best all-around resource for dealing with people with drinking problems. Their number is 1-888-4AL-ANON (1-888- 425-2666).

Move the Protective Wall/Act in Your Own Interest—Protecting your kids is more important than protecting your mom from her behavior. Make a pact with your spouse or partner that your mother is not to be left alone with the kids.

Refuse to Keep Secrets—If your mother asks why she can't take the kids, tell her the truth in a calm clear voice. Inform your cousin with kids about your mom's drinking and driving.

Problem

Your cousin is siphoning money from the family business. No one else seems to be aware of this.

Seek Help—Discuss this with the company lawyer. Talk things over with a trusted advisor.

Move the Protective Wall/Act in Your Own Interest—Change access to the accounts. If your cousin must have access, require two signatures on each check.

Refuse to Keep Secrets—Turn over any proof of your suspicions. This is not to send anyone to jail, but to keep you out of the conspiracy.

Problem

Your brother has gotten involved with drugs. You're not sure if he's dealing, but he's edgy all the time.

Seek Help—Drug laws vary widely from state to state. Consult a legal advisor to make sure you and your family don't become embroiled in his problems.

Move the Protective Wall/Act in Your Own Interest—Keep your kids away from him and his house. His kids can play with yours at your house.

Refuse to Keep Secrets—Don't make excuses for him and don't lie to your parents about him. Don't hold packages from him or run errands for him. Don't loan him your car.

EXERCISE:
HANDLING PREDATORS AND TYRANTS

Now you can map some options for yourself. Think of a situation where you might have to deal with a family member who might hurt you or others. Remember, it doesn't matter whether or not you find him charming or feel sorry for him. It only matters that he presents a danger.

Know Your Predator

Predation or tyranny includes:

1. Physical, sexual, or emotional abuse

2. Felonies

3. Rage seizures with physical violence

4. Forcing others to lie for him or her

5. The bell jar effect (an isolated circle of silence)

6. Jekyll and Hyde behavior

Can you think of a conflict where a relative displayed Jekyll and Hyde behavior? What was she like in public? How was she different in private? List her behaviors in your notebook. Use the format shown below.

In Public   **In Private**

_____   _____

_____   _____

Compare your lists. What do they tell you about how your relative really is? What do they tell you about how your relative needs to be seen?

Write your observations in your journal or notebook.

Now, think about the bell jar effect, the powerful circle of silence. Has it appeared around this person? When? What was it like? How did it keep you or someone else from getting help?

Write down your answers in your journal or notebook.

EXERCISE: OLD PATTERNS

Now we're going to shift the focus to how you may have become caught in these traps. As these problems were taking place, you would have been expected to act out a certain role. For example, in the past, you might have exhibited some of the following behaviors:

1. An inability to act in your own interest

2. Abetting the lies of others

3. Protecting felons rather than protecting yourself or your dependents

4. Rage seizures of your own

Consider whether any of these behaviors were practiced by you in the past. Don't worry about blaming yourself. These practices are defense mechanisms that don't work very well. These defenses won't be helpful to you now, so you'll want to be aware if they come back.

If you have engaged in any of the above behaviors, list them in your journal or notebook. Then describe how these behaviors appear in your life now.

EXERCISE: NEW PROTECTIONS

Now that you're an adult and you can feel the bell jar effect forming, think of some ways that you might break the bell jar. Some examples might be refusing to be alone with this person and walking out the door, refusing to keep his secrets, or calling 911.

What are some ways you might break the bell jar? Write your options in your journal or notebook.

This time, think of how you might release a secret you no longer want to carry. Think of a responsible friend or professional you might discuss this with. Why would this person be a good choice? What would you need to discuss? Write your choice of person in your journal or notebook.

Now, think of how you might redraw the family circle so that you and your family are protected from the predator. For instance, you might arrange for a separate place to sleep if this person starts drinking that night, or plan a trip to the movies if you don't want your children exposed to ugly behavior.

Write down your solutions in your journal or notebook.

These options give you a range of different ways that you might take back control of your life.

CONFLICT AS UNDERTOW

Growing up under tyranny or predation can have very long-lasting effects. These conditions seem to create an undertow effect that can affect your life long after the abuse stops. You may insist that your past is all ancient history and you shrugged off the effects a long time ago. At the same time, you may be aware that you don't enjoy stable, caring relationships, or you drink too much, or, somehow, happiness seems out of reach, no matter how hard you try. Effects like these could just be coincidence, of course, or they could be the result of earlier childhood abuse.

Predation causes deep damage to individuals within families, especially to children. These are not the kind of wounds that are easily treated at home by yourself. This kind of damage requires industrial-strength treatment. Even if you think you're doing fine and have gotten over things, please consider making a commitment to see a professional counselor or attend an experienced support group. This can include:

1.   Counseling

2.   Al-Anon

3.   Domestic violence support groups

4.   Sexual abuse survivor groups

If you really are fine, invest in a few sessions and see if your assumptions about your mental health are true. If, instead, you are merely numb from your childhood experiences, you will finally have a chance to get your life back. You are worth the time and effort.

If you're contending with an undertow, you need to become a good swimmer. You may need a swim coach, in the form of a skill-based counselor. Or you may need to join a swim team, in the form of a solid support group.

Olympic swimmers don't win medals by themselves. They have coaches and belong to swim clubs; they are constantly improving their technique and polishing their skills. Ordinary swimmers can just muddle along, but muddling along will not give you what you need to get out of an undertow. You'll need stronger skills, better judgment at spotting riptides, and ongoing awareness and discipline. Of course it's work, but it's well worth doing.

You may not want to engage in therapy or find a support group because that's only for losers. Show me an Olympic swimmer who didn't have a coach and I'll agree with you. Now, you may have encountered support groups that didn't have many skills; they just whined a lot and felt sorry for themselves. Those aren't skills you need, so find yourself a better swim club. There are some excellent swimmers out there, and you need to learn from them.

Chapter Six

Calming the Family Storm

It's easy enough to escalate conflicts without meaning to, but it's possible to de-escalate them as well. This chapter covers common conflict patterns with an eye to calming family storms. This assumes that the conflict in question doesn't involve an extreme situation like an active predator. Those are deep-rooted problems, not temporary flare-ups. Someone who is addicted to crack or alcohol will not listen to reason or negotiate in any meaningful way. This chapter focuses on less toxic issues.

This chapter will be useful for learning how to deal with:

- Everyday conflicts

- Temporary snags and flare-ups

- Repeating family patterns

- Long-term conflicts that don't cross into abuse

These techniques are not designed to cover:

- Domestic violence

- Child abuse

- Sexual abuse

- Psychiatric disorders

- Felonies or serious crimes

FAMILY TRIGGERS

It's all too easy for things to go wrong when you call or visit your folks. What you'd hoped would be a pleasant conversation goes bad, and you both come away with mixed feelings of anger and self-pity, somehow combined with guilt. You may also be mystified at how or why your call or visit went so badly so fast.

You probably touched on a family trigger. Remember, it's normal for people's behavior to move up and down on the Conflict Continuum. Triggers spark the shift. Unexpected triggers appear in the best of families; we will never be entirely free of them. Instead, the goal is to become aware of common triggers in your family and to work around the trip wires. Rather than just react when things go wrong, you want to be ahead of the game.

PRIMATE SIGNALS

You may have an elderly relative, perhaps your grandmother, a tiny woman, who can walk into an argument and quiet the crowd with a glance. Or you may have a soft-spoken uncle whom everyone respects, and who never has to raise his voice to be heard.

These are people with natural authority. They have a presence, a certain confidence that makes other people respect them and consider their opinions. They can interject a note of sanity and calm into contentious situations, and do it without even having to breathe hard.

How do they do it? And more to the point, how can you learn to do it, too?

These quiet authority figures may have uncommon good sense and courage, but they transmit their calm by means of signals that date all the way back to our primate ancestors. Gorillas and chimpanzees don't use words, but communicate by using body language. That language has been passed down to us; we respond to it instinctively. In fact, if there's ever a contradiction between what you say and what your body language conveys, your gestures will be believed while your words will be discarded. It's like someone who snarls, "Alright, I'm sorry!" It's certainly not taken as an apology. The tone of the snarl says it all.

Did you ever tell your three-year-old niece she had to behave, only to have her run right over you? Ever insist that your brother had to listen to you, only to have him brush you off? Odds are you said the right things with the wrong body language.

If you are going to set boundaries, negotiate, be respected as an adult, or accomplish any of the changes you want to bring about with your family, you need to get your body language right. Get this aspect of communication right and your life will become easier. Get it wrong and these nonverbal signals will undermine everything else you try to do.

I first learned these signals from Nanci Newton, who worked at a domestic violence shelter while studying primatology at the University of Wisconsin. A petite woman, Newton not only had to negotiate with devilishly difficult families, at times she had to toss abusive husbands out of the center. Rather than wrestle with someone who might outweigh her by a hundred pounds, she would turn on her gorilla signals and walk the surly man out the door.

Here, we'll cover three types of signals:

1. *Authority signals.* The ace-in-the-hole of your tiny grandmother and the uncle whom everyone respects. This is what you want.

2. *Belligerence signals.* Aggressive gestures designed to either scare people or provoke fights. This is what you don't want.

3. *Submissive signals.* These are the gestures of the frightened, timid ape. These signals can get you run over, even by little children.

Authority Signals

Authoritative posture is calm and direct. You stand with upright good posture, and direct a level, steady gaze at the other person. If that person scares you, never let it show. Look between his eyebrows, if his eyes are too intimidating. He won't be able to tell the difference.

Take all the emotion off your face and relax your hands. Don't sprawl, but take up all the room you need.

If you need to convey maturity and authority, don't smile. Check out pictures of Nobel Prize winners: at the pinnacle of their careers, one of the happiest moments in their lives, they're not smiling. That's the face of authority.

Keep your voice low and resonant. If you have a naturally high, breathy voice, work on your low register. Children have high, breathy voices, and you have to make it known that you're not a child anymore.

Authority signals include:

- Upright posture

- Facing the other person directly, with no part of your body turned away

- Comfortable, steady stance

- Expressionless face

- Low, resonant voice

Think of all the American icons of authority: the judge, the gunfighter, Superman. They plant their feet firmly on the ground, make eye contact with a clear gaze, show little emotion, and stay rather still. They don't sprawl or look up at the ceiling.

If you need to set a boundary, speak up for yourself, or make an apology, do it while holding the authority posture.

Belligerence Signals

These are the intimidating cues of a bully. Think of a snarling pit bull: the jaw juts out, a ridge of muscle lowers over the eyes, and the growl comes out in a low, guttural snarl. These are the signals of a dangerous dog about to bite. Bullies depend on these cues to do half their work. But just because they send these signals doesn't mean they're actually impressive; they'd just like you to think so.

Bullies, after all, are often bluffing. In apes, full belligerence is not necessarily the sign of the ape in control; often, it's more the ape concerned about losing status. The dominant ape who is completely unchallenged does the calm, steady stance, not the snarling belligerence.

Belligerence signals include:

- "Bulldog" look: jutting jaw, ridge of muscle over eyes, teeth showing in a snarl

- "Charging bull" posture, with head thrust forward and looming body

- Bashing things

- Shaking a finger in someone's face

- Snarling, barking voice

When you are facing someone doing the belligerence posture, do not be impressed. If you show fear, she'll only get worse, and she may just be a thundering gasbag. Examples of belligerent displays in the family may include:

- Slamming a door

- Slamming down books or packages

- Peeling out in a car at top speed

- Shaking a telephone or utility bill in your face

These are all displays, designed for maximum effect. Don't buy into them.

Now, if you have genuinely wronged someone, you may also get a belligerent display. If your father is shaking the phone bill in your face because you ran up $400 in charges at his house, you need to pay that bill. He's entitled to be angry and he wants your attention. The same issues apply: he's concerned about losing control of $400, as well he should be. So solve the problem: apologize and pay the bill.

When someone snarls and thunders at you, your first response may be to snarl and thunder back. Don't. Belligerence only provokes more belligerence. Authority signals are what work.

Submissive Signals

Submissive signals are the nonverbal cues of the small, timid ape. If you, as a human, convey submissive signals, you may be considered weak, childish, or even stupid. You have got to divorce yourself from these signals.

Submissive signals include:

- Hunched, huddled posture

- Self-clutching—for example, clutching your own arms, twisting your hands

- Fidgeting

- Fearful grin

- Foolishly animated face

- Toying with hair or jewelry

- Jingling coins or playing with keys

- Fluttery clothes or dangling jewelry

- Clinging to objects

- High, breathy voice

Any bad situation will be made worse by a submissive posture. Let's say you scratched the family car and need to apologize to your father. If you apologize in a submissive posture—ducking your head, fidgeting or smiling foolishly—he probably will jump all over you. However, if you approach him in an authority posture—body standing tall but relaxed, steady hands, looking him squarely in the eye—he'll probably accept your apology and talk with you about how to get it fixed.

People displaying submissive postures are assumed to be weak, cowardly, stupid, and even dishonest. In humans, these are the signals of someone who deserves a good thrashing, and angry people are predisposed to deliver exactly that.

Don't tempt them. Erase submissive signals from your nonverbal vocabulary.

GAUGING A SITUATION

Since few people are really aware of their nonverbal signals, the following offers a quick way to assess a situation. Conflict, after all, is fluid. You need to know if the situation is changing, especially if it's changing for the better.

Consider Eric's experience with authority signals. The last time Eric saw his brother, he had a terrible fight with his sister-in-law. They hadn't spoken to or seen each other since. He dreaded seeing his sister-in-law again. He never wanted to fight like that again. However, the family was gathering for the holidays, and Eric had to be there. He was prepared for the worst.

He had coached himself in ape authority signals and the process of de-escalation, wanting to cool down any opportunity for a fight before it started. As he came off the ramp from the plane he saw his brother and sister-in-law in the crowd. She was hugging herself and smiled up at him with an anxious grin: clearly, she was in a submissive posture. Eric realized she was as worried about him as he was about her! She didn't want to fight any more than he did.

Instantly Eric knew what to do. He relaxed into a friendly version of the ape authority posture and greeted his sister-in-law. He was outgoing and warm toward her, and he made many small gestures to reassure her. He did everything he could to reinforce her belief that she needn't fight him, that they could get through this visit in peace, and they did.

PUTTING IT ALL TOGETHER

These types of signals feed into existing family patterns. Consider what reputation you need to live down and how you wish to be seen in the future.

These are a few of the family associations:

- Belligerence: Surly teenager, spoiled brat

- Submissiveness: Inept child, hopeless loser

- Authority: Competent adult, a credit to the family

There's one last aspect of these signaling systems to keep in mind. If even one small submissive or belligerent cue leaks out, it can undo the entire effect. Think of the steely lawman at high noon—with one foot nervously dancing around or his hand white-knuckled, grasping his badge. He suddenly looks like Barney Fife, trying to pretend to be tough.

You must be thorough. Think about your gestures when you're angry or nervous. Do you unconsciously clench your fists? Pull on one earlobe or fiddle with your watch? Know your own signals and get them under control.

Solutions: Nonverbal Cues

Problem

Your parents still treat you like a child.

Solutions

Do: Stand up straight or sit up straight.
       Look them calmly in the eye.

Don't: Wear any jingly jewelry or fussy clothes.
       Wear sloppy clothes that don't fit.

Problem

Your parents dismiss your opinions without a second thought.

Solutions

Do: Use a low, resonant voice.

Don't: Argue.
       Veer into belligerence.
       Whine when you try for their attention.

Problem

Your parents treat you like a surly teen.

Solutions

> *Do:*   Sit upright on the furniture.
>   Take one body's full amount of space in the room.

> *Don't:* Sprawl all over the furniture.
>   Put your feet up on the furniture.

EXERCISE: NONVERBAL CUES

Visualize someone you have known who had a quiet air of authority, someone others instinctively respected. It might be a teacher, boss, or respected elder. They may not have been physically powerful, yet they conveyed a personal power that others found both calming and benign.

Now, a marine drill sergeant might be imposing, but you don't want a barking belligerence. That will trigger a new fight at home. Instead, picture someone calm and powerful. For instance, a grandmother may sit in her chair as if it were a throne. A particularly effective boss might walk into a situation—any situation—and look alert and capable of dealing with anything.

Picture that person clearly in your imagination. Now, physically move into that person's persona. How does he sit in a chair? How does he stand? How does he make a request? Give an order?

Try to adjust your voice tone to match that person's. Use your hands as he does. Practice stepping into his shoes, so that you feel comfortable adopting his style by the time you see your family again.

VULNERABILITY

You might think anger would be the quickest route to family conflict, but it's not. Instead it's vulnerability. We love our families and, of course, we want their attention or approval, but when things don't go well, those desires leave us vulnerable.

Suppose you drive up in a new car, or wear a new coat, or arrive with a new date. Your mom looks up from her knitting—and sniffs. Then she goes back to her knitting. You may feel a turmoil of emotions, angry, or hurt, or indignant, all because you wanted a touch of approval. If you didn't care what she thought, you wouldn't be upset. And as vulnerable as you are to your parents' opinion, it's not as if they're exactly averse to annoying you.

Families have uniquely provoking ways. You brave subzero temperatures and travel six hundred miles through a blizzard, only to be ignored by your father in favor of his aging Chihuahua. You had hoped to talk with him a little, perhaps fill him in on your promising work toward a cure for cancer. Your father, however, is unimpressed. He tosses a frozen dinner your way while he lovingly toasts chicken necks for a creature that looks like a mutant rat.

You try not to let on that you feel competitive with the dog, if only because it's humiliating to admit you come in second. As annoyed as you are and as vulnerable, your father need do little more than forget the name of your company to trigger a terrific fight.

When he fumbles for the name (you've only worked there seven years), you jump over all over him. Your feelings of vulnerability have led you to overreact and commit a social violation: ridiculing him for a trivial mistake. Then it becomes his turn to feel insulted, so he counterattacks and cuts you down to size. His feeling of vulnerability spawns a new violation.

The pattern looks like this:

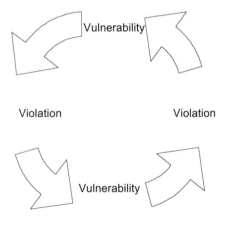

Vulnerability

Violation   Violation

Vulnerability

Violations

Violations usually appear in one of three ways. Family members may become:

- Aggressive (which includes sarcasm)

- Controlling

- Withdrawing

For instance, suppose you're about to go out to dinner with your family and your father looks at you and feels a flash of anxiety that others won't approve of your clothes. He feels vulnerable, so he gruffly says, "You can't wear that jacket. Here, put this on," and shoves a different coat at you. He's being controlling. That's a violation; you are no longer a child to be dressed by him.

You, in turn, feel mortified and offended at the thought of wearing something out of the back of your parents' closet. This is a vulnerability. Rather than just say no, you make fun of his clothes, which becomes a new violation. So, your father feels vulnerable and takes offense, and says you can stay home for all he cares. That slam becomes a new violation. And so on around the circle. Examples of controlling violations include:

- Nitpicking at perceived flaws in your hair, body, or speech

- Pressuring you to change clothes, makeup, or your whole appearance

- Limiting where you go or who you meet

- Bribery or flattery

- Playing off one family member against the other. ("Your brother doesn't hang out with losers. Why do you?")

Controlling violations can escalate to outright aggression. Examples of aggression include:

- Unkind teasing

- Subtle or unsubtle criticism

- Punitive withholding, such as taking away house keys, or refusing an agreed-upon ride to the airport

- Insults and yelling

When this pattern is in play, you might not think to handle these violations directly. Instead you might withdraw in some essential fashion. But withdrawing generates its own brand of tension. Examples of withdrawal include:

- Not answering phone calls

- Traveling 2,000 miles to be with your parents, then spending the entire time watching TV

- Being "busy" the entire length of your visit

- Moving to a distant part of the country to get away from them

- Self-isolation/pushing away affection

- "Ghosting" (being so emotionally detached you aren't really there)

Keep in mind, if you're dealing with an active predator, withdrawing or sealing yourself away can be a sensible way to protect yourself. However, if you are around more normal family members, withdrawing is apt to be upsetting and trigger a new round of frustration and vulnerability.

Vulnerability and Anger

Because vulnerability is such an uncomfortable feeling, it's apt to be translated into anger. Anger can feel pleasingly self-righteous. This explains many family quarrels that otherwise make no sense at all.

For instance, Ferrel's parents were elderly and beginning to have health problems, even though they were fiercely independent. With considerable patience, Ferrel had helped them sort through different living situations that could suit both their medical conditions and their independent spirit.

Ferrel was feeling hopeful that things would work out, when he was surprised by a vicious e-mail attack from his brother. It was so weird that, at first, Ferrel didn't react at all. He didn't know what to think. He'd done nothing to antagonize his brother and things with their parents seemed to be moving along well. Thinking, perhaps, the e-mail was just a fluke, Ferrel ignored it, but soon he started receiving waves of angry e-mails, all arriving first thing in the morning.

Ferrel was hurt and ready to retaliate. He already had his hands full with their parents and he didn't need this. But he happened to notice that all of these furious e-mails were sent between midnight and 2 A.M.

Think about it. In the middle of the night are people prone to fits of righteous anger, or waves of fear and loneliness? These inexplicable, savage e-mails were just a form of panic attacks. His brother was afraid of what was happening to their parents, and Ferrel happened to be the only one available to attack.

In fact, the family had a long-standing pattern of lashing out when they felt scared. It didn't matter that Ferrel was the one who was handling the problem. His brother was scared and flooding, so he attacked.

Ferrel's brother's vulnerability led to a violation. And if Ferrel didn't control himself, he would counterattack, which would only create a new vulnerability. That would lead to a new violation, and they would be going around the circle all over again.

SOLUTION: SKIP THE VIOLATION. SET A BOUNDARY

Rather than getting bogged down in this endless cycle, the solution is to set a boundary rather than create a new violation. That is to say, control your flooding and don't retaliate. Instead, set limits.

Ferrel informed his brother that he wasn't going to put up with these attacks anymore. He told his brother that if he had something to say, he could be civil about it. Moreover, Ferrel made it clear that if he got any more e-mails dated from the middle of the night, he was going to delete them unread.

His brother's daytime e-mails became much more reasonable. In time, he apologized obliquely; he wouldn't say he was wrong in so many words, but he made conciliatory gestures. So Ferrel's approach worked. Lashing out would not have solved the problem, but setting a boundary did.

A dozen ordinary, everyday violations could trigger the same cycle. Examples include:

- The family know-it-all who corrects you about your own field of expertise.

- The family member who exhibits an interfering sort of "concern": "I'm just worried how you'll ever get a job with that tattoo."

- Your mom who tries to "help": "Why don't you have a look at these clothes in this catalog? C'mon, honey. Black just isn't your color."

- Feigned ignorance: Your sister looking mystified at there being no gas in the tank after she borrowed your car.

- Infuriating timing: "I know you've got to go right now, but could you just have a look at my computer?"

- Not listening.

- Your brother smiling knowingly about your ex-boyfriend.

EXERCISE: BREAKING THE OLD CYCLE

Take a moment and picture a family trigger that can spark a reaction from you. Of course, when you think about this trigger, you're likely to flood, so start by breathing deeply and bringing your adrenaline down.

Now, in your journal or notebook, write down some common family triggers that are likely to set you off.

When you finish writing, think about the triggers you just named. How do they hit your vulnerable places? For instance, when your sister feigns ignorance about using up all your gas, it might not be about the money. It may trigger the feeling that she takes advantage of you, or remind you of the years she got away with being irresponsible while you had to clean up after her.

Think about these vulnerabilities or sore points. Then, in your journal or notebook, write down which of your vulnerabilities are triggered at these times.

Next, think of how you would normally defend your vulnerabilities. For instance, you might complain and withdraw in a huff when your sister uses up your gas, or make a verbal jab at your brother when he gets that knowing smile. Sulking, sarcasm, retreating, or counter-attacking would all be ways to defend a sore point.

Think about how you defend yourself after someone in your family has hit a sore spot. List your usual defenses in your journal or notebook.

Now you have a log of your usual pattern. The old approach probably hasn't worked very well or you wouldn't be reading this book. So, at this point, you might try something different.

For instance, let's say in the past your sister would use up all your gasoline. In response you huffed and complained. She looked sheepish and tried to jolly you. Then the next time you saw her she'd do it again, which is a form of payback for your being so churlish and such a sap.

Since that pattern doesn't work, think about how you might swap your normal form of counterattack and, instead, set a boundary limit. For example, instead of griping about your sister using up the gas, you can explain how you feel and then take back your car keys. Or you can ask for gas money up front, before lending her your car, especially if she has a better job than you do.

Here's another example: instead of grumbling and fuming when your mother makes last-minute requests as you walk out the door, have her write down a list of what she needs done, and e-mail it to you before you come to visit. That way you can plan accordingly and have the right tools on hand. If she sends you a list of forty-five jobs, you can ask her to mark her priorities.

Instead of either avoiding her or scolding her for being so impossible, set new terms in a reasonable way. If she ignores your boundaries (as families often do), don't get mad but hold the line. Insist that you're fine completing small jobs, but she has to warn you ahead of time. Don't do the work. Put it on your list for later.

Think over your usual triggers, and consider how you might swap a counterattack for setting a new boundary. Write down what your new approach will be in your journal or notebook.

MONITORING SIGNALS

When your mother sniffed at your new car and then went back to her knitting, or your brother gave that knowing smile about your date, you may have felt a sudden flash of anger. You also may have felt oddly embarrassed. Also, you might have wondered why you even reacted, since neither one actually said anything. The reason for your reaction is that the sniff or knowing smirk were actually monitoring signals.

Monitoring signals are quick, virtually subliminal gestures that express disapproval. They work roughly like a psychic rabbit punch; you hardly see them, but they hurt. These subversive gestures were first documented by Scheflen and Scheflen in their book *Body Language and the Social Order: Communication as Behavioral Control* (1972). While studying videotapes of troubled families, the Scheflens discovered non-verbal signals that were so powerful they altered family behavior as if a flag were dropped.

For instance, a troubled teenager might have veered dangerously close to revealing a family secret, and a parent would sigh and look away in a show of exasperation. Then the teen would stop talking. These were not particularly obedient kids; they were often teens in a lot of trouble. Yet they obeyed the nonverbal cue in a way they would never obey a command, and the conversation could be steered back to safer topics. Later if the teen approached the land mine again, the parent would give a slight, disapproving cough, and once again the teen would let the matter drop.

Neither parent nor teen seemed aware they were doing this. In fact, the Scheflens didn't even notice the pattern until they had studied the tapes repeatedly.

Some signals were openly insulting, like rolling the eyes or giving an exasperated sigh. Other signals, like glancing away or a quick brush of the nose, were hardly noticeable but turned out to be every bit as powerful as disapproving coughs or sighs. Now, here is a list of monitoring signals:

- The God-you're-stupid sigh

- Looking away

- A slight cough

- Smirking

- Rolling the eyes

- An insulting laugh

- Brushing the nose

Smirking is an open insult, but brushing the nose is more unexpected. If someone rolls his eyes and laughs at you, you can't miss the contempt. But a quick brush of the nose turns out to have much the same impact.

With monitoring you don't quite know what hit you. You may know Aunt Lydia has a wicked way of crushing your pride, but it's hard to say exactly how she does it. She's always unfailingly polite, and she never raises her voice. Yet you dread being in the same room with the woman; you come away feeling cut to pieces. But she's said nothing, so you may end up feeling as if there's something wrong with you. You're not crazy. She's probably using monitoring signals.

The Purposes of Monitoring

Monitoring can be used to:

- Crush dreams

- Enforce conformity

- Shame you into obedience

- Control others without resorting to persuasion or open requests

For instance, in these contentious times, your family may be split along political lines. If your politics don't match your family's, you may voice an opinion only to have all your relatives roll their eyes or silently laugh. You feel humiliated. You're apt to either lash out or fall silent, feeling that any further communication is hopeless.

Those are the two most common ways to react to monitoring: either becoming suddenly angry or abruptly withdrawing. Yet if you show your temper, your relatives will behave as if your reaction came from out of left field:

You: "I don't need this flak. Who do you think you're smirking at!"

Your brother: "Hey, chill, I wasn't doing anything. What's your problem, anyway?"

Now you're doubly shamed: first you aired a controversial opinion, and now you're picking on your brother. Monitoring can get you coming and going.

Although an angry reaction is pretty overt, feeling suddenly abashed and embarrassed is more internal. You may fail to notice if you drop what you're doing, even if you happen to be engaged in something both right and necessary. Let's say you're trying to get your sister to repay a loan:

You: "Sherri, we need to talk about the money you owe me."

Your sister: "What again?" (Deep sigh)

You're apt to feel chagrined, as if the wind's been taken out of your sails. A moment ago you may have felt indignant and determined; now you feel embarrassed by your own impertinence. Only there was nothing wrong with your behavior; you were asking for your own money. Yet, under monitoring, you lose your momentum and fail to press for the money.

Solution: Bring Monitoring into the Open

Monitoring is an unspoken weapon, operating just below our level of awareness. Rather than allowing it to control you, you might consciously note the sign, file it for future reference, and then go ahead with whatever you'd originally planned to do.

You: "Sherri, we need to talk about the money you owe me."

Your sister: "What again?" (Deep sigh)

You: "Yep, cash it is. Can you pay me now or do we work out a payment plan?"

Once again, you want to avoid the cycle of violation and vulnerability. You don't lash out in anger or pull away and sulk. Instead you set a boundary: time's up for the loan. Let's work out a plan for how it'll be paid back.

Another alternative might be to stop the conversation and talk openly about monitoring. For instance, if you were monitored about your politics, you might say, "Jim, you just rolled your eyes at me. If you don't agree with me you can say so, but rolling your eyes is not fair play."

Your brother may be unaware of what he's just done. For instance, Jim's reaction to your statement is likely to be to roll his eyes up to heaven again. You're free to use this as a teaching moment. You say, "There—just now, you rolled your eyes again. That's a signal for contempt. Remember Uncle Marv? He used to do that all the time, especially when we caught him cheating at cards."

Practically speaking, you may as well stop and talk about monitoring signals, because with such things going on you're not going to get very far on politics. With monitoring signals in play you'll only insult and provoke each other. If you want to teach your brother to drop monitoring, you'll likely do better with a less loaded topic, like Uncle Marv.

By talking about monitoring openly, you strip away its hidden power. It may still sting, but you've broken its ability to control you blindly.

Now, you may have a relative who is wedded to dirty fighting, who will never stop monitoring. Rather than accept it, you can pleasantly call it out. If she keeps rubbing her nose and sniffing, ask if she has allergies. If her favorite monitor is a slight cough, ask if she's coming down with something. Bring the behaviors out into the open. Discuss it with your other siblings ahead of time. You are probably not the only one getting this treatment, and they might be curious to know what's going on.

In the middle of monitoring, you can also take the dispassionate approach. Why not enjoy a good family fight? In a crashing good family fight with monitors flying left and right, you might just keep a running tally of who is monitoring whom, and how. It will keep you sane when everyone else is losing it.

Meanwhile, if you're in the habit of monitoring others, you need to become aware of what you're doing and give it up *now*. This is wickedly unfair fighting, and you can permanently undermine the trust and goodwill of people you love. Monitoring alienates people and can drive them away. You might disagree with people, argue, persuade, or reason, but do not monitor. It's simply too damaging.

If, by the way, you are reading this and making plans to secretly monitor a sibling or two, forget it. Researchers found monitoring signals could not be faked. The Scheflens tried using actors. Either the monitoring was the genuine article or it had no effect at all.

GUILT LOCK

Shaming signals, quite naturally, bring us to the topic of guilt, which is the internal version of shame. Guilt lock explains one of life's great mysteries: how you can feel so bad about a given event and still do nothing about it. *Guilt lock* is the emotional equivalent to gridlock, and it is just as paralyzing.

Let's say you really love your grandmother and you know she'd like to hear from you. You mean to send her a card or call—but you don't. Time passes. It really bothers you that you haven't called or written, and yet you still do neither. Your nagging guilt turns up at odd times, when you're falling asleep or driving to work, but the fact remains that, even though you're increasingly feeling ashamed of yourself, you somehow never call or write.

After a while you've let this slide for an inexcusable length of time. You feel terrible about it; other family members have started to make comments, and, still, somehow, you don't do it.

You're not a miserable excuse for a human being. You've hit guilt lock.

Guilt lock springs from a little known fact of human nature. We think of guilt as a motivator, yet often the opposite is true. Researchers found that when we feel guilty, rather than act, we tend to avoid whatever it is that made us feel guilty. (I cannot locate the sources of this insightful study; if a reader does know, please tell me so proper credit can be given in future editions.)

Doing nothing naturally leads to more guilt, which creates more avoidance, which creates more guilt, until we are thinking about the problem all the time and can't bear to do a thing about it.

That's guilt lock.

Guilt lock can be triggered by the following situations:

- Thank-you letters you forgot to write

- Invitations you didn't send

- Visits or phone calls you never made

- Favors you didn't return

- Any inattention to a parent or family elder

Any deeply felt obligation can end up creating guilt lock. Family interactions tend to heighten the effect. Families involve a thousand small commitments, many of which we may have bungled. Once we've messed up, we feel embarrassed; feeling embarrassed, we begin to avoid things. Soon, again, guilt lock.

Part of the problem is that families routinely make each other feel guilty. Guilt is used as a tool, particularly as a motivator for kids. When you were in your teens and your mother wanted you to take out the garbage, she got on your case until you felt guilty enough to do it. When you were a teenager, it worked—sort of. It also required your mom to nag you endlessly until you took off the headphones and hauled your indolent butt down the stairs with a sack of overflowing trash.

The catch is that the guilt required a good deal of nagging to actually get you moving. As an adult, the internal nagging can leave you locked in place. Guilt lock can create otherwise inexplicable conflicts that embroil the entire family.

For example, Philip was a young man who moved back to his hometown where most of his family lived, after a job transfer hadn't worked out. He was low on funds and he didn't have a car, so he borrowed his mother's. He soon found a job and bought his own car—but he didn't bring back his mom's car. At first, it was just a matter of juggling obligations, but the more embarrassed he felt about having his mother's car, the more he avoided returning it. The more he avoided, the more ashamed of himself he became. Soon Mom was annoyed, his siblings were angry with him, and all the while the two cars sat in his driveway.

There were no drug or alcohol issues, Philip wasn't short on money, and there was no practical reason for him to act that way. But by then, he was so ashamed of his own behavior that he couldn't face his family. He didn't understand himself why he had acted this way, and so he continued feeling terrible and watching too much TV. He'd hit guilt lock.

One of his brothers figured out what was going on, and intervened. First, he telephoned his brother and brought up the subject of guilt lock. He asked, could that be the problem? Philip described feeling a wave of relief; he'd been thinking that he had just turned into a rotten human being.

Just having a name for the problem was a help. Then the two made plans for the next Saturday. They got the oil changed, washed and waxed the car, picked up a bouquet of flowers, and delivered the car to Mom.

Solution: Taking Action Breaks Guilt Lock

The good thing about guilt lock is that once you act, the worst is over. It's *not* acting that's the killer. Do anything useful at all to break the paralysis, then follow up with your next move before it gets another grip on you. Once you act, keep acting. Momentum is the key.

Here are some tips for breaking guilt lock:

- Remind yourself that you are neither crazy or worthless. You've hit a common human glitch.

- De-escalate the pressure. Quit calling yourself names and turn off the guilt-inducing tape in your head. You need to be less guilt-ridden, not more.

- Write down steps of what you need to do. Don't worry if they're not in order—you may be flooding and may have trouble with sequence. Just write down all the steps that come to mind.

- Next, choose one or two of the steps to get started. Choose something you can manage emotionally. For instance, if you need to write thank-you notes for your wedding (now eight months past), you can make a guest list or buy stamps.

- Give yourself a deadline for starting on the core issue, like committing to writing ten thank-you notes by Wednesday.

In building momentum, it's fine to start small. Also, it may help to have a friend with you in the room while you do these things. It may sound unnecessary to need a buddy around while you write out thank-you notes, but it helps to have someone on hand in case you freeze up again. Your friend can tackle part of the work or just hang out and read a book. Your friend's main job is to keep you calm and in motion.

EXERCISE: BREAKING OUT OF GUILT LOCK

Think about the kinds of things that leave you feeling so guilty you stop acting at all. You can choose a current example or one from your past. The triggering event may not even be anything major. It could be as important as visiting a sick relative in the hospital or as minor as not returning a phone call. Yet large or small, it triggered paralysis when you needed to act.

Write down your triggers for guilt lock in your journal or notebook.

Now that you know about guilt lock, think about a first step that might snap you out of it. For instance, if it's a phone call you haven't returned, plan how you might start the conversation. (If it's really been that long, you might start with an apology.) Then, have a friend or relative nearby so that you actually pick up the phone and make the call.

Write down a few "first steps" that would feel manageable enough for you to do. List them in your journal or notebook.

Now, look over the "first steps" you set out for yourself. Put a star next to the one that's most important to you. Right now, pick a good time to do it, such as this weekend, or next Tuesday when your cousin will be visiting you.

The key to beating guilt lock is to take the plunge and follow through. It's like a toothache. Putting off dealing with it is far more painful than actually handling it.

FOOD IS LOVE

Do you need to help snap someone out of guilt lock? Bring food. Any difficult discussion you need to have will go better if you have something to eat and share.

Food is both a powerful symbol of family unity and a useful tool for solving conflicts. By its very nature, food is calming and reassuring. In cultures all around the world, friends and families eat together, while enemies do not. That imprint is so powerful it has been used to save lives in hostage negotiations (Kennedy 1993).

For instance, if a gunman calls for a sack of burgers, savvy hostage negotiators will not comply. Instead, they'll send in a loaf of bread, some meat, and mustard and ketchup. The reason for that is the gunman won't be able to put down his weapon and fix a sandwich himself. The hostage will have to do it for him, and is likely to join him to eat. If the hostage prepares food and the two eat together, the gunman is far less likely to kill the hostage. The peacemaking message is that powerful.

If you need to de-escalate a family conflict, "breaking bread" together is a good idea. Your best choices are hands-on, casual, messy food. Think pizza or ribs at home or in the backyard, rather than a formal sit-down meal at a restaurant.

For maximum effect, prepare the food with your own hands or share it from one large platter. For instance, you could grill some trout on the barbecue, with extra points if the fish were caught by Uncle Ray. As you hand out the food, tell some stories about Uncle Ray or fishing.

Other homey, communal foods include:

- Barbecue, especially if you hand it out hot off the grill

- Family-sized bowls of homemade potato salad or greens

- Stews or chili

- Roast turkey or anything carved at the table

- Pies or cakes, especially from a family recipe

- Bowls of shared snacks, like popcorn or chips (Pass the bowl rather than doing separate servings.)

- Any food that's traditional in your family, particularly if it's prepared in a kettle or casserole

If your family has a tradition of sharing fast food, get a bucket of chicken or ribs and share that. Better yet, start a tradition or revive one from your past.

If you have a bridge to mend or a difficult topic to broach, bring it up tactfully after you've eaten together. It will help if you also have some communal work to do, like helping with the dishes or straightening up after the meal. At a time like that, your words will go down easier, and any apology is more likely to be accepted.

Food and Change

Because eating food together is so bonding, it can create a special problem should it have to change. Food is a core symbol of tradition. Family occasions are built around food: especially traditional recipes like Grandma's special string beans or cookies from the old country, (even if the old country is Porter County, Indiana).

Yet sometimes food has to change. Betsy, who had been struggling with her weight, went back to visit her family: "I'd been doing so well, avoiding white flour and white sugar. Then I went home, and my mother was just pulling a loaf of white bread out of the oven. On the sill was a rhubarb pie."

She added ruefully, "I'd been doing so well. . . ."

It isn't necessarily that your family intends to sabotage your diet. It's more that family food is such a powerful symbol that most people feel it should be eternal, even when it's bad for you.

A family's food is a way of declaring identity. A Polish family eats pierogies and potato pancakes, properly served with a side of sour cream. A Nebraskan family serves sausage and bacon with eggs. It might clog up your arteries, but it's a bone-deep way to declare family unity: this is who we are.

Turn vegetarian and your family may go into shock. Your family does not think of the welfare of Bambi or Elsie the Cow; your family thinks you've become something foreign and they will strive to change you back.

This can create some strange scenes. If you're a dieter desperate to lose fifty pounds, your family may welcome you warmly, hug you and comment on how great you look, and then sit you down to a table of bacon and sweet rolls. If you've been diagnosed as diabetic, they may show their love by serving a "lighter" version of Grandma's pecan pie.

This may seem like a contradiction. They declare their love for you while trying to do you in. Perversely, the more worried they are about your health, the more they may insist on family treats. They're afraid for you. Food is soothing. Have some ribs.

Unfortunately, this can set off a weird kind of loop. The more you refuse, the more alarmed they become, and the more they may try to force-feed you. If a family member is desperately ill and unable to eat, they may puree fried chicken to be sipped through a straw. It's revolting, yet really rather touching. The family is valiantly fighting to take care of its own, even if it kills them in the process.

This kind of problem is best headed off in advance. Call ahead, explain what's going on, and talk about some food you'd really love to have. Give them some direction to show their love. If you're vegetarian and your family is carnivore to the max, find something—anything—that's family and acceptable, if only three-bean salad or baked potatoes. Then bring a casserole of your own you can trust. You'll do better if you can somehow relate it to family history. If you're trying to get along, this is not the best time for Tofu Delight. It could be the time for a riff on Granddad's famous lasagna, secretly adapted for vegans.

Do not be so foolish as to ask them to adapt a family dish. Frightening things can happen: veggies sautéed with baco-bits, a perfectly roasted vegetable plate made with just a touch of lard. Thank them kindly. They're showing that they love you, even if it's maddening. Be tactful, but come prepared.

Food Is Love

The key to understanding is to recognize that families show their love through food, even if they can't express it any other way. Saying "I care about you" may seem too strange and foreign, so they do the equivalent by laying in a year's worth of Snickers bars.

Some of these food-as-love gestures can seem a perfect mystery. A new daughter-in-law once visited her husband's crotchety dad, who proudly pointed out there was a five-pound mason jar of honey on the table. She didn't know what to think, until her father-in-law reminded her that the last time she came to visit she had had trouble opening the honey jar. Now the honey was in a container with a wired latch and a four-inch mouth, in a jar big enough to be opened by a bear cub. She'd forgotten about the whole thing. But it was food, so he'd noticed and planned for a new jar to make her feel at home.

She would have been happier if had he smiled once in a while or even said good morning. Instead he offered her a massive jar that could be opened without opposable thumbs. The gesture meant "You're welcome here." So, say thank you and admire it, no matter how strange it is.

EXERCISE: DE-ESCALATING FAMILY CONFLICTS

Problem

You're back at home for the holidays. Your sister and you are locking horns over one trivial issue after another.

Solutions

Primate Signals—You know you're annoyed, so check your body language to see whether you are antagonizing your sister unnecessarily. Is your jaw locked when you talk to her? Are your fists clenched? Get rid of some of your angry gestures and she may cool down a bit.

Monitoring—In a similar way, do you roll your eyes when she makes a suggestion? Does she sigh at your helpful hints? Get rid of your own monitors first, and use that as an opening to ask her to get rid of hers.

Food—Ask her out for pizza. Make dinner with her. Sit up late watching old movies, sharing a bowl of popcorn.

Problem

You were the kid who was always the screwup. Ten years later, no one will let you break out of that role.

Solutions

Primate Signals—If you were the dumb screwup, get rid of any trace of submissive signals. If you were the surly screwup, divorce yourself from belligerent signals. Hold strictly to authority gestures. Intentionally sit up straight. Keep your hands on the table and your feet on the floor. Look people in the eye and lower your voice. Be prepared for people to ask if you've started working out lately.

Monitoring—If you were the traditional screwup, people probably monitor you reflexively, which may make you inclined to feel either angry or beaten before you start. Notice the monitor, but do not react. Turn all your ape authority on that person. Get up and walk around. See if you don't see a marked decrease in monitoring over the next few days.

Food—Help someone in your family prepare food, and use the time to talk about your new life. Win them over one on one. Some will be more comfortable in the morning fixing breakfast; some late at night over snacks. Someone else may be working outside; fix him or her a sandwich and bring it outside to talk, if you have a bridge to repair or a difficult topic to broach.

Chapter Seven

Direct and Indirect Language

We'll start with a brief quiz. Choose the answer that seems most like something you might say. If neither choice is quite what you'd say, just pick the one that fits best. Please circle your answer below, or write down your choices in your notebook or journal.

1. Your mother casually mentions a terrible idea, like having your drunken uncle climb out on the roof to fix some loose tiles. In trying to talk her out of it, you say:

    (a) "Oh Mom, you can't do that! No, no, no, no, no."

    (b) (Thoughtfully) "I don't know. Isn't cousin Jerry working part-time these days?"

2. You want to write a note and you realize your pen is across the table, next to your father. Do you say:

   (a) "Could you hand me my pen, Dad?"

   (b) "Dad, is that my pen by your elbow?"

3. Your brothers are organizing a flag football game. You're not in the mood. Which of these is the best way to say no?

   (a) "No thanks."

   (b) "Why don't you ask Dad?"

4. You'd like your sister to return the bulky wool sweater she borrowed from you a month ago. You say:

   (a) "Sis, could you bring my sweater when you come by?"

   (b) "You know, it's really getting chilly in the evenings these days. We've been keeping the thermostat down. I swear there's nothing around here that quite keeps the chill off . . ."

5. It's just before noon. Your sister calls to ask you for lunch, which is her homemade tomato aspic. You haven't had lunch, but you loathe tomato aspic. You say:

   (a) "Sis, I'd love to come over, but why don't I pick up some takeout? I'm just not that big on tomato aspic."

   (b) "I'd love to come over, but I've already eaten. Why don't we just have coffee?"

Now, in your notebook, write down the total number of times you chose answer (a), and the total number for (b).

   (a) _____

   (b) _____

If you primarily chose answer (a), you are a direct speaker. This means you communicate by saying exactly what you mean, no more, no less. You would be surprised to learn that some people find you rude, abrasive, and insulting.

If you primarily chose answer (b), you are an indirect speaker. This means you tactfully imply what you mean, trying to anticipate the other's response and doing what you can to avoid giving offense. You would be surprised to find that some people think you're manipulative, sneaky, and maddening. What's more, people often have no idea what you're talking about.

If you are one of the few who are equally likely to choose (a) or (b), you can speak both direct and indirect language. You are one of the few people who can translate easily between these warring camps.

DIFFERENT LANGUAGES

Your first reaction might be to insist that the quiz and its results are ridiculous; no responsible adult could possibly choose (a); that is, unless you feel equally sure that (b) is the only possible answer. However, linguists have identified two different forms of English in America, direct and indirect languages. Both exist, even though each version seems absurd to the other.

If you don't believe me, do this simple test. You must know someone who speaks primarily in the alternate fashion. Show that person the quiz. See if he or she doesn't choose the opposite set of answers than your choices, and watch him or her respond with the same incredulity to your choices.

This difference has been known to linguists for some time, but it was popularized by Deborah Tannen in her two landmark books *That's Not What I Meant!* (1984) and *You Just Don't Understand: Women and Men in Conversation* (1989).

Some psychologists hold that indirect speech is a sign of manipulation, even dishonesty. Linguists, however, disagree. Linguists hold that these two forms of English are simply different and legitimate ways to communicate. There is some evidence that women are more likely to use indirect speech than men, but this may be outweighed by personal or cultural factors. For instance, the Japanese are largely indirect speakers, as are middle- and upper-class Brits. America, with its diversity of culture, is more of a mixed bag.

Now, you may suspect your entire family speaks directly or indirectly, as you do. Given the cultural component, that could be true. If everyone in your family speaks alike, you are welcome to skip this chapter. However, you may find this language difference exists with colleagues, neighbors, or friends; in that case you may want to read this chapter.

Direct speakers may find these translations unnecessary and perplexing. Perhaps you can't imagine that communication can be so involved. If so, please keep reading. You may discover that a family member isn't so plainspoken after all, or that other people, perhaps at work or in your neighborhood, have been throwing you linguistic curveballs that your family never prepared you to handle.

This chapter has two different goals. One is to help direct speakers learn to examine how their words can be misinterpreted, and even how some communications may have gone right over their heads. The other goal is to help indirect speakers with the problem that they speak a language that many others don't understand.

"Directs" need to pick up enough rudiments of the indirect form of language so they can function better with users of indirect speech.

"Indirects" need to learn that others aren't ignoring them or willfully antagonizing them. Rather, much of what indirect speakers say is thoroughly misunderstood. Indirects need to learn enough about direct speech to give these people the chance to cooperate with them.

Indirect to Direct

Indirect speakers usually understand each other well, and the same is true of two direct speakers. The trouble starts when these different types try to talk with each other.

Let's look at a common, loaded case: Suppose your mom wants you to have children. Here's how she would put it in indirect speech:

Mom: I saw Marge the other day. Did you know that her son and daughter-in-law just had another baby?

(Translation: When are you going to have kids?)

Mom: The new baby is so cute! It was wonderful to hear Marge talk about her grandchildren and how happy she is!

(Translation: Where's my grandkid? I want a grandkid!)

Mom: She told me that her daughter is finally feeling fulfilled. She also said that after all those years of raising her own kids, she feels she's finally being rewarded with her own grandchildren.

(Translation: You rotten ingrate. After all I went through with you and your brother, you can come up with a kid.)

Mom: Today, everyone at the bridge club was passing around pictures of their grandchildren. Well, except me, of course.

(Translation: I feel like a loser because of you. I can hardly face my friends.)

Mom: Marge asked me if any of my kids were married.

(Translation: She was asking whether my children are complete social misfits. Do you know what it's like to eat crow around that miserable woman? And you're the one who's doing this to me!)

Now, if Mom was talking with a grown son or daughter who is a direct speaker, she may have noticed something remarkable: nothing got through. She might as well have talked to the dog. Her son or daughter will have munched contentedly through their meal, nodding at significant pauses without the slightest comprehension of what she was talking about. She got no better response than "I remember Marge. How's she doing these days?"

To an indirect speaker, this can be maddening. She'll believe this obliviousness must be a sign of defiance, because no one could be that dense.

Meanwhile, direct speakers may notice that Mom is slamming cabinet doors and tossing glasses into the dishwasher overhand, so they know she must be worked up over something. What it could mean or why she's upset remains more or less a mystery.

Indirect to Indirect

Compare this to a more lively situation, where an indirect mom is addressing an indirect daughter. The daughter knows exactly what Mom's saying and quickly joins battle:

Mom: Marge was just over here showing me pictures of her grandchild. What a beautiful baby!

(Translation: Where's my grandkid?)

Daughter: Did her daughter ever marry that guy? What was he, a bookie?

(Translation: We don't have any kids because the two of us were finishing college. Isn't that what you wanted?)

Mom: Oh, he's in sports, but never mind him. It's the baby who's a beauty.

(Translation: Don't change the subject. You've had plenty of time since college.)

Daughter: Do they still live in Marge's basement?"

(Translation: We're waiting until we're financially sound. Why do you even listen to these losers? Why can't you be proud of who I am?)

This conversation is no longer a monologue but a regular fencing match. Meanwhile, any direct speakers in the room will have no idea what they're talking about, or that a battle's taking place.

DIRECT PRESSURE

Arm-twisting is by no means confined to indirect speakers. Direct people can do just as well, including using unfair tactics. They'll just be more terse and to the point. Here's the same kind of pressure from a direct mom:

"So what's with you not having any kids? People are starting to talk, you know. You want to have them while you're still young enough to enjoy them. *I* want to be young enough to enjoy them. Is it too much to ask that I should hold my grandchild before I die?"

Although direct speakers would get to the point immediately, indirect speakers would find the second mom lacking in finesse, and consider her lecture in very bad form. Indirects would find the direct mom's speech the verbal equivalent of beating someone over the head with a blunt object. They might agree wholeheartedly, but would never agree to say it that way. To them, it would feel like a loss of face to engage in such bald strong-arm tactics.

Misunderstanding

On the whole, indirects consider direct speakers abrupt, pushy, rude, dense, and spoiling for a fight. After all, who would talk this way if they weren't trying to provoke a confrontation?

At the same time, direct speakers tend to consider indirects underhanded, manipulative, dishonest, and grossly unfair. They feel that indirect speakers are always expecting them to read their minds and jump through hoops just to engage in a simple conversation.

In fact, one way to identify direct speakers is that after a fierce encounter, sometimes they can be found in a corner, muttering, "What was that all about?"

Indirects don't ask these questions. Not only that, when direct speakers do ask, the indirects don't believe them. Instead, they're convinced it's all an act. They believe the direct speakers must understand what they're saying, they just don't want to admit it.

These core misunderstandings cause a great deal of unnecessary conflict. It's very hard to work out solutions if you annoy the other side every step of the way.

But it doesn't have to be that hard. Here are some guidelines for translating these two forms of language and staying out of trouble.

MAKING YOURSELF HEARD

Indirects often feel as if they're rudely disregarded by directs. Actually, the case is more that they never heard the direct speaker's opinion in the first place.

Let's say, for instance, that an indirect speaker and a direct speaker are making plans for the holidays. The indirect loves corn bread stuffing. Lobbying for her favorite, she says, "Don't you think corn bread stuffing is perfect for the holidays?" The direct speaker thinks a moment and replies, "I dunno. Not really."

The direct translation reads: "I've never thought about corn bread stuffing." The indirect translation reads: "Corn bread stuffing is stupid. And so are you."

The indirect speaker believes that her feelings have been rudely overruled. She may start to indignantly praise corn bread, cite the relatives who love it and its place in family tradition. The direct speaker looks blank and shrugs, going back to his work. After all, how much time can you spend discussing corn bread stuffing?

The indirect speaker now feels doubly slighted. Why should she put up with this kind of treatment from her own family? Meanwhile, the direct speaker may have no idea that there was an argument, much less that he was part of it. If later he claims he hadn't understood, the indirect will feel even more offended, because it is clear to her that now he's playing stupid.

In all these breakdowns, direct speakers may feel that they've been put in a hopelessly no-win position; the whole thing seems grossly unfair. Indirects, meanwhile, feel they are overruled at every turn, and they just want their feelings considered once in a while.

Direct speakers will, in fact, consider an indirect person's feelings. But first, they have to hear what they are. If you're an indirect speaker, it's best to make yourself known in simple terms: "Actually, I like corn bread stuffing. Aunt Jeannie used to make it and I miss it at the holidays. Why don't we do corn bread this year?"

The direct speaker is entirely likely to say, "You like corn bread? Hmmm. Dad likes savory. What if we have a pan of each?"

Now, to an indirect speaker, giving her opinion in so many words seems rude and high-handed. She sees it as an attempt to impose her will on others. Direct speakers don't feel that way and are unlikely to take offense unless they are addressed in a really surly tone of voice. They won't see it as a coded test of the relationship. To direct speakers, corn bread is just corn bread—no context, no deeper subtext. They'll probably be relieved to know what it is that's wanted.

Setting Boundaries

Another place where problems crop up is when indirects try to set boundaries. If it's not put into plain words, the direct speaker won't even hear it.

Let's say an indirect speaker wishes to have his family come over for a visit, but he doesn't want to put up with his brother's Chocolate Labrador. It's a nice dog but unruly, and the last time it was over it dug up the garden.

Not wanting the dog, the indirect brother says, "I don't know if your dog's comfortable here." Now, a Chocolate Lab is comfortable anywhere outside the polar ice caps, so the direct brother says, "Oh, he'll be fine."

The indirect brother says, "Really, I wouldn't want to inconvenience you," and the direct brother says, "It's no inconvenience. He'd love the ride."

To set a boundary with someone who is a direct speaker, you don't have to get mad but you do have to be specific: Say, "He's a nice dog, but he tore up my garden last time. Please don't bring him over."

Again, in indirect speech that is horribly confrontational. In direct English, it's just a statement of fact. The direct speaker will then try to think up ways to keep the dog from destroying your garden, or leave it home, or work out some other arrangement. But none of this can happen until he actually hears the words.

Context

Indirect language depends heavily on context. Understanding this helps explain otherwise mystifying conversations.

For example, Sally, an indirect speaker, was about to get married. She was getting dressed, and wore her hair shoulder-length, as she always did. Her mother, another indirect speaker, came in just as Sally was about to put on her wedding gown and said, "Are you wearing your hair down?"

The bride laughed lightly and said, "I guess so."

A few minutes later, Sally apologized to her mother for snapping at her. If you were a direct speaker, you would have had no idea a conflict had taken place.

This scene was witnessed by a direct-speaking sister, who normally would have been clueless. But think of the context: it was to be a big ceremony, and it was a few minutes before Sally was to put on the gown. Every detail had been planned for months. For her mom to come in and question the bride's hairdo could only mean disapproval.

The entire encounter would have been far less graceful in direct speech:

Mom: You're getting married with your hair like *that?*

Sally: Yup. Deal with it.

You must admit that indirect language is certainly more tactful. Indirect, after all, is the language of diplomacy.

Sniping

Diplomats also know how to be mean, which is another fine art in indirect language. Indirect speakers can excel at sniping, particularly as an "us against them" tactic. Only insiders would understand the layered meanings, while an outsider would be puzzled and made to look like a fool.

For instance, one large Italian family used to haze any woman Phil brought home, particularly if she wasn't Italian. One of his aunts might pass the food, saying, "Honey, I don't know if you've ever had food like this." It was a bowl of spaghetti.

It's context again. Of course anyone would have eaten spaghetti. It was code for "You are so not Italian, and we don't know why Phil dragged you in."

Now, a direct speaker might be mystified as to why anyone would think she'd never eaten spaghetti. A direct guest might stumble through a puzzled response, not knowing what to think. An indirect sniper would delight in this, showing up the outsider to be dim, oafish, and inept.

A more socially adept response might be to be pleasant and firmly refuse to see any hidden meaning. Kill them with kindness: "Why Mrs. Lucha, I'm sure I've never had spaghetti like yours."

This puts the indirect person in a quandary. First, it would be churlish to refuse such a compliment. Second, it isn't entirely clear that it's a compliment at all. Is it that you've never had such food because nothing you've encountered has tasted so bad? Either way, it will give them pause, which is what you want from a sniper.

You might also have a pleasant stock line that you adhere to relentlessly. For instance, when you're not sure if a comment was meant well or not, you can pleasantly say, "Aunt Myrna, you're such a card."

In indirect speech, there are a few layers to that. First there is the resolute refusal to acknowledge that anything unpleasant was meant. Indirect snipers don't necessarily like being misunderstood. This will give Aunt Myrna the choice either to become bolder and more straightforward (and risk coming out into the open), or to give up entirely and stop sniping since it doesn't seem to be working.

The other layer is that calling someone a "card" may not be exactly a compliment. Jack Benny was a card, like other comics from the forties or fifties. Young, hip people are not "cards," only aging people who tell corny jokes. However, if she stops taking shots at you, you can stop calling her a "card."

Similar quasi-compliments would include "you're a real cutup!" "aren't you something!" and "you're so cute."

A Compliment or Not?

What is a welcoming gesture in direct English can be perceived as an outright slam in indirect. For instance, Frances, a minister's wife, was a truly sweet-natured woman. She came in on three of her younger relations, two of them dressed nicely while the third was wearing some motley sweats. Frances smiled at the third and said, "Don't you look comfortable."

In indirect, that would mean, "What a slob!" But Frances meant it in the best way possible.

The ambiguity of indirect language can serve to cover unfair fighting. Another phrase open to misuse is "God bless 'em." The pattern is to say something absolutely awful, and then add "God bless 'em." As in: "She never did manage to marry that boy she was chasing. Expect she'll have to deal with the baby now, God bless her." Or: "Those children just run around half-starved and half-naked, God bless 'em."

You can split these sentences into two halves: the first part, which is vicious gossip, and then the clincher "God bless her" (or him, them, or it). The second part is supposed to make the first part alright.

Direct speakers will find this puzzling, and they would be unsure of what to think. Indirects would listen for tone and intention. Is there disapproval? Smugness? Glee? Are there monitoring signals? Does the speaker quickly heap on more dirt? All these point to the "blessing" as a slam.

A genuinely good-natured use of "God bless 'em" may use a tone of voice that says, "There but for the grace of God go I." Or the phrase might have an indulgent tone, as when referring to a favorite, eccentric uncle: "So he cleaned up that awful looking dog and took it home, God bless him, and wouldn't you know it was sitting on his porch last Tuesday looking like it owned the place."

When you split that sentence in two, you don't have ugly gossip, just a quirky story about a nice old guy.

Gifts

With direct speakers, a gift is a gift. With indirects, gifts can carry more symbolism than the Japanese royal court.

Suppose you ask your mother what she would like for Mother's Day. She replies, "Oh, nothing dear. It's the thought that counts."

In direct speech that means your gift-giving will be easy, and she will be pleased with anything pleasant or thoughtful.

In indirect speech, your gift-giving will be difficult, because the proof of your affection is that you know her so well that you will figure out what she wants without being told. Guess wrong and you're in trouble. Guess right and you've only passed that test.

Directs believe this kind of communication to be a form of torture, designed to ensure they'll fail. They think it's a sadistic game. Since there's no way to win, they just go through the motions of gift-giving, convinced that they'll get it wrong no matter what they do.

Indirect speakers are not necessarily being cruel. Instead, they find it rude and distasteful to bluntly declare what they want. They may feel that would be on a par with saying, "Gimme that." Instead, indirects are apt to offer tactful clues, so that you can refuse without anyone losing face. For instance, an indirect speaker may pause at a shop window and say, "Isn't that a lovely chair? Can't you just picture yourself in a chair like that?" If it's one week before her birthday, this means she wants that chair.

The indirect will believe she has made her wishes known. If you then bring her a box of chocolates, she'll be annoyed, thinking you heard her, and then deliberately overruled her feelings. Of course, then the direct speaker will compound the insult by failing to notice that anything's wrong.

In contrast, if you ask your direct-speaking father what he wants for Father's Day, he may say, "Oh, nothing. We've already got too much crap around here." His statement may be accurate, but it might be wise to hedge your bets. He may not want anything else to gather dust in the garage. Instead, you might get him a service or something disposable.

Gift possibilities include:

- A chit for one day of cleaning out the garage

- Two tickets to a ballgame

- Washing and waxing his car

GIFTS AS COMMENTS

Gifts also can be indirect tools for broaching delicate topics. Here are some examples:

Indirect mom: Have you seen this new face cream? I really love it. Do you want it?

(Translation: You look awful. Do something about your appearance.)

Indirect dad: I hear there's a great new acrylic wax out these days. Has a coating like armor.

(Translation: It's time to wash your car.)

"THAT'S INTERESTING."

This statement is not a compliment from an indirect person. "That's interesting" is an all-purpose phrase used when an indirect speaker is uncomfortable and can't stay silent. Meanings can range from "Lame!" to "That's revolting."

Sometimes the remark is frankly mystifying to a direct speaker. For instance, on learning that a teenage cousin is pregnant, an indirect person might say, "That's interesting." Now, that particular situation can be many things: upsetting, disastrous, heartbreaking, exciting, but "interesting" doesn't even begin to cover it.

The worst-case scenario occurs when the hapless direct speaker hears "that's interesting," and then keeps on talking, since, clearly, he or she has finally found a topic that interests this distinctly hard-to-fathom individual.

Take the case of two middle-aged cousins, one of whom has discovered a new and exciting activity:

Direct: Yeah, me and the hubby just signed with a nudist colony.

Indirect: That's interesting.

Direct: Really, you do meet interesting people there, and they can really be themselves without their clothes on—well, you know what I mean.

Indirect: That's lovely, I'm sure.

Direct: I'm not sure 'lovely' is exactly the word I'd use, but . . .

So, you can see that direct speech has its own form of torture, as the indirect speaker tries to exit a desperately unwanted conversation.

ANGER

Anger poses a special quandary for indirects, since one of the main goals of indirect speech is to show no sign of outward aggression.

Directs have no such problem. Here is a direct speaker on learning her unmarried daughter is pregnant:

"What were you thinking? Do you want to ruin your life? Do you realize what people are going to say?" And perhaps adding the topper: "You're only doing this to get back at your father."

An indirect speaker, however, may not be able to blow off steam by simply throwing a fit. Such bald statements would be considered a shameless loss of control. Yet at some time in everyone's life, everyone has to lose it. To get her anger across, an indirect person may have to resort to passive-aggression, such as slamming cabinet doors or radiating unspoken hostility.

An indirect speaker may also voice her anger by blaming herself: "Where did I go wrong? Didn't we give you enough love as a child?"

Then the indirect person must be consoled: "Mom, you were a great mom."

"I must have done something terrible for you to do this."

You may have to take some lumps before you can get to the point: "Mom, I know you're upset, and maybe you raised a dumb child. But maybe you raised a smart one, and maybe I know what I'm doing. At least you could tell me you hope for the best."

With indirects, sometimes the message is in what *isn't* said. Here is a mother talking about her unwed daughter's pregnancy:

Indirect: Well, your father handled it well.

Not said: As for me, I considered slitting my wrists.

Indirect: Your father's delighted.

Not said: I feel humiliated, absolutely sick.

Indirect: Your father's always been very supportive.

Not said: Your father's an idiot.

Confusion

Unfortunately there are times when even indirect speakers get it wrong. With all their sophisticated language skills, even they hit awful moments when they realize not only have they been misunderstood, they have also upset or offended someone.

Sometimes the only way you can tell that something's wrong is when you realize someone is avoiding you.

George, a thirty-five-year-old man, was chatting with some cousins he hadn't seen lately, and suggested that they should get together some time. His cousins had a vacation home in the area, a very nice place with a pool. Since they had mentioned it was hard for them to get away, he offered to make the trip to visit them. After a few days, George realized that not only had they not responded, they were now avoiding his calls.

George made two mistakes here. In indirect speech, when a couple says it's hard for them to get out, it often means they've turned down your invitation. It's their way of saying no without giving offense.

His second error was with the context of the conversation. They had been discussing vacations and property and George realized too late that his cousins believed he wanted to camp at their place. But he had no desire to impose; he just wanted to get to know them again.

In such a case, George might call back with a clear and neutral reason for his call, one that would soothe any fears of imposing.

For example, George might say to his cousin, "Alex, I was thinking about putting in a pool at my place, and I was wondering if you could show me around your setup. I've been talking to salespeople lately, and I'd like to get the straight story from someone who knows."

This clearly says George wants advice. Advice is flattering. His cousins would no longer have to wonder what he wants. If he spells out a specific project, they won't have to worry about what's up his sleeve.

CRISES

You may face a family crisis where well-meaning strangers use indirect speech to spare your feelings. They may be so careful and use so many euphemisms you have no idea what they actually mean, even though your vital interests may be at stake.

For example, on the last day of my mother's life, my brother and I were at the hospital listening to the doctor's prognosis. She'd had a heart attack the day before and wasn't particularly alert. It was up to my brother and me to handle things.

The news was not good, so it was delivered in what was meant to be a thoughtful, caring manner. In fact, it was so mystifyingly oblique that after the doctor left, my brother turned to me and asked about the next course of meds. But there were to be no meds. My mother was about to die and we had just agreed to move her to the hospice.

That, however, was the direct translation. The actual phrases the doctor used were more like these:

"We could order more tests, but I'm not really sure there's anything meaningful to test for."

(Translation: Tests have already shown her heart is damaged beyond repair.)

"Perhaps it's best to make her comfortable. There's space upstairs in the hospice. Has she ever discussed her wishes with you?"

(Translation: She's dying and there's nothing more we can do. Our hospice is much nicer than this. Did she ever discuss what she wanted near the end?)

My brother is another direct speaker like myself, but he wasn't schooled in the language difference. That entire conversation went over his head. He had no idea what he had just been told.

The doctor didn't intend to be obscure. She meant to be tactful and kind, but she did so in a language my brother didn't understand.

Other professionals may use indirect language, such as social workers, nursing home staff, ministers, and funeral directors. Meanwhile, at such times you and your family are apt to be flooding, so your language skills will not be at their best.

So, instead of agreeing to something you may not understand, anticipate. Beware of any euphemisms. If you aren't perfectly clear what the doctors are saying, keep asking for clarification until you're sure you have it. You can respond to the doctor by saying, "You say, 'It's best to make her comfortable.' Does that mean we should take her home?"

Or you might say: "Everyone's suddenly become very tactful. Just how bad is it?"

Doctors and other professionals may never question their indirect language, but they are used to conversing with families who are in a daze. If you keep asking for clarification, they will find a way to get through to you.

Solutions: Direct and Indirect Language

Direct and indirect language can produce a world of misunderstandings. You may feel that any civilized human being will talk as you do. This won't happen. It's best to be prepared for the difference, because it won't go away anytime soon.

Here is an overview of solutions for both direct and indirect speakers.

TIPS FOR DIRECT SPEAKERS

■ Phrase things more "gently" around an indirect person. Use more words to pad your sentences.

■ Ask the indirect speaker to explain in a five-word sentence.

■ Ask her to write down items in bullet points. She will have to be concise and to the point.

■ Say, "I seem to be having trouble here. Could you try that in plain English?"

■ Have an indirect friend translate. If no one's available in person, you can always call and turn over the phone.

■ Finally, if you simply can't understand what the indirect speaker is saying, make a guess that's deliberately wrong and let him correct you: Say, for example, "So this means the crisis has passed and we can take her home in a few days?" The indirect person will then have to spell out exactly what's going on.

TIPS FOR INDIRECT SPEAKERS

■ If a direct speaker doesn't seem to understand you, shorten your sentences.

- If you're short and to the point, you aren't being rude. In fact, a direct speaker is apt to feel relieved.

- Take all statements from direct speakers at face value. If you can detect no sign of hostility, there probably is none.

- A direct speaker's idea of courtesy is to say "Please" or "Thank you." Do not take offense unless you're quite sure offense is intended.

DIRECT AND INDIRECT EXAMPLES

Here are a variety of ways to handle direct and indirect breakdowns.

Direct Problem

Your mother did not give you a clear answer about what she wants for her birthday. You know these things matter to her, but you don't know what she wants.

Direct Solutions

Give her the benefit of the doubt.   Indirect people can be particularly uncooperative about gifts or favors. This isn't because your mother is trying to make you crazy, but because indirect speakers feel the vagueness is tactful and even thoughtful. She probably means well.

Look for context.   Watch for some uncharacteristic statement on her behalf, like stopping and admiring pottery in a shop window or commenting on a neighbor's flower boxes. This is her way of signaling what she wants. If you get the signal and it turns out not to be what she had in mind, she'll still give you credit for paying attention and for being thoughtful.

Leave an opening.   If you want to confirm whether she really wants these things, start a conversation later about pottery or flower boxes at a hypothetical friend's house. If she waxes enthusiastic, she's interested. If she changes the subject, she's not.

Indirect Problem

You and your extended family all use the family lodge for vacations. You all take turns helping out, but your older sister takes the lead on gardening. You would like to see some zinnias. So you said to her, "Zinnias are nice, don't you think?" and your sister shrugged. It doesn't look like you're going to get zinnias.

Indirect Solutions

If your sister is a direct speaker, keep your phrases short and to the point.

Try saying: "I like zinnias. Could we put some in? I'll help."

Check to see if you were understood.

Does your sister look hostile? Does she look as if she's deliberately ignoring you? If you don't pick up any signs of anger or resentment, she probably isn't stonewalling you. She probably doesn't understand this matters to you.

Adjust your idea of courtesy.   If your sister is a direct speaker, she won't think you're being rude by being plainspoken and frank. She'll prefer it.

EXERCISE: COMMON COMMUNICATION SNAFUS

From the quiz at the beginning of this chapter, you learned whether you are a direct speaker or an indirect one. Now, think of a time with your family when you seemed to miscommunicate. (If you and your family all speak with the same habits, feel free to do this exercise by thinking of a family friend or neighbor.) Think of what you were trying to communicate. Write down your intended meaning in your notebook or journal.

Now, think of how you might translate your meaning into the opposite language. If you need to, look back at the bullet points on the previous few pages. Remember, you're translating, so at first this may feel a little awkward.

Write your translation in your notebook or journal.

This time, think of how you might set a boundary by speaking in the opposite style. Let's say you need to tell a relative that you don't want to go out to the movies tonight.

If you normally speak indirect, you will have to keep your words short and to the point, adding only "please" or "thank you" to show you mean well. If you normally speak directly, you might phrase things more gently than you usually would, or pad your sentences with extra words.

Now, write your boundary statement in your notebook or journal.

Chapter Eight

Villains, Victims, and Heroes

The syndrome of villains, victims, and heroes was first mapped by the great family therapist Virginia Satir in her book *The New Peoplemaking* (1988). The pattern is made up of three roles. First there's the victim, who is perhaps wronged and usually feeling sorry for him- or herself. Next, there's the villain, who wronged the victim. Finally there's the hero, who will step in, defeat the villain, and save the victim.

This seems reasonable enough on the surface. After all, victims, villains, and heroes are characters in the time-honored plot used in everything from Italian spaghetti westerns to fairy tales with princesses and ogres. But Satir noticed that something awful happened when you forced real people into ogrish roles: that is, all the players switched roles.

For instance, in chapter 4, we described Bill, a young man who worked in his family's restaurant. Bill was upset at his mother for yelling at the restaurant's employees, so he decided to set things straight.

We could sketch that situation in this way:

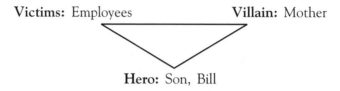

Victims: Employees   **Villain:** Mother

Hero: Son, Bill

So, Bill came to the employees' rescue and when his mother started to yell, he began yelling at her. This attempt at peacekeeping quickly backfired, as his mother then turned on him.

From his mother's point of view, the pattern looked like this:

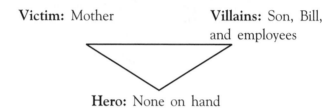

Victim: Mother   **Villains:** Son, Bill,
                                        and employees

Hero: None on hand

When Bill's mother became more incensed rather than de-escalating, Bill retreated in defeat. So then he became the villain and his mother ruled as villain.

However, the role of the hero was left vacant, so some family member or long-term employee is apt to be pressed into service either to pacify the mother or take the son aside and counsel a more tactful approach. However, if the new hero isn't careful, the mother, son, or both of them will turn on him or her as a meddler. So the triangle keeps turning.

We could do a similar quick sketch showing the same dynamics with the grandparents who wanted to take their grandkids on a trip to Disneyland (see chapter 3). That's a generous offer, a hallmark of a hero. But by making an end run around the kids' parents, they cast the kids as victims, held back from happiness by their unfeeling parents. Mom and Dad were cast as villains who would deprive their kids of the chance of a lifetime.

We can sketch the start of that conflict like this:

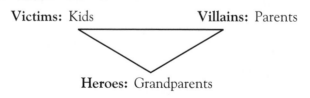

Victims: Kids   **Villains:** Parents

Heroes: Grandparents

What was initially just a pleasant offer quickly turned into a melee. Once the parents learned of the scheme, they hit the ceiling. They played out their role as villains and verbally lacerated the grandparents. Now the grandparents were hurt, and they became the new victims. The kids, meanwhile, stepped in to intercede with their parents, which made them tiny heroes. Their parents, however, would have none of it and shot down any interference in a hurry.

So the next round looked like this:

Victims: Grandparents   **Villains:** Parents

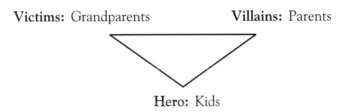

Hero: Kids

Meanwhile, the parents didn't feel very villainous at all. They felt like victims themselves, beset from all sides and thoroughly underappreciated. They called up their siblings to complain about what impossible grandparents their parents were turning out to be. From the parents' point of view, the conflict looks like this:

Victims: Parents   **Villains:** Grandparents

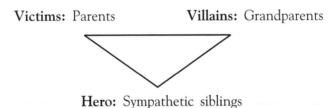

Hero: Sympathetic siblings

This pattern doesn't generate a lot of happiness. The grandparents feel misunderstood and beset, while the kids are upset as the grown-ups war around them. So everyone ends up feeling like a victim, and everyone can point to a villain.

This is standard family chaos: the roles stay the same, but the cast keeps changing. Of course, if a sibling actually intervenes, she will find herself in a hornets' nest, fated to become the next victim in the never-ending dance.

This was Satir's brilliant insight: Once this pattern starts, all the roles switch. All sides become enmeshed in a game they can't win. They might have a brief moment of glory as heroes, but quickly enough, they will fall from grace.

Notice the speed with which these roles switch. In the case of both Bill and the overreaching grandparents, they changed from hero to villain nearly as soon as they opened their mouths.

THE TRIANGLE NEVER STOPS SPINNING

Satir called this the "Toxic Triangle," and she saw it as a tempting trap. Once the pattern starts, there is no stopping it. Any number of family events may trigger the spin. For instance, the fairy-tale bride (a hero) might morph into Bridezilla the villain. Or else, beset by her family, the glorious bride can even become a victim at her own wedding.

Here's a selection of common family roles that can spawn a Toxic Triangle:

Victim roles:

- The overwhelmed son (or daughter)

- The misunderstood, unappreciated kid

- The helpless parent (even when he or she is pulling strings)

- The adult kid whose "Life Was Ruined"

- The beleaguered bride

- The family mooch

- The family martyr

- Any stepparent

Hero roles:

- The perfect son (or daughter)

- The dutiful daughter (or son)

- The child who will "Right the Wrong"

- The beautiful bride

- The kid who sticks up for Mom (or Dad)

Villain roles:

- Anyone wishing to marry the perfect son (or daughter)

- The no-good kid

- The controlling parent

- The parent who "Ruined Your Life"

- Bridezilla

- Any stepparent

The Risks of the Hero

You can see how easily these roles change. The perfect son becomes the overwhelmed son, and if he collapses under the weight of his responsibilities, he becomes the villain everyone's mad at.

A heroic effort also can trigger the family spin. For instance, suppose one kid drives through a harrowing snowstorm to visit the family at the holidays. (Or his heroic effort might be a long plane flight, or even a properly exaggerated bus ride across town.)

The kid arrives, tired and bedraggled, and would like to receive a warm welcome or even an offer to sit down. Instead he walks into the usual, which may be:

- An embarrassingly fussy parent

- Everyone bickering about something meaningless

- Someone else getting all the attention

So the kid, who would have liked to have scored some points as a hero—or at least as a loyal family member—feels thoroughly let down and rather sorry for himself. Now, he's the victim. So, feeling a bit sullen and testy, he picks a fight with his nearest sibling over any topic of choice. Now he is the villain, and the triangle has turned again.

Of course we all want to play the hero for our families, but Satir discovered this doesn't work. In this syndrome, the hero inevitably gets pulled off his pedestal and ends up in trouble. The problem isn't being a hero. The problem lies in the pattern itself.

EXERCISE: VICTIMS, VILLAINS, AND HEROES

Think how the members of your own family play out this pattern. For instance, your father may feel upset about your mother's spending, so he becomes sarcastic. He feels like a victim, so he turns into a villain. Your mom, in turn, feels like a victim because she takes the brunt of your father's anger. To defy him she racks up more bills, which makes her a villain. The kids will be lobbied to take one side or the other, which makes them heroes, until, of course, someone's anger is turned on them.

Now, either in the space provided below or in your notebook, sketch in some toxic triangle roles that play out in your family. Note how roles switch around.

Victim: _____   Villain: _____

Hero: _____

Victim: _____   Villain: _____

Hero: _____

Don't be surprised if you can't name a hero. Heroes can be so short-lived that this role can stay unfilled at times.

Now, certain behaviors go with each role. For instance, when Dad feels like a victim, he starts muttering to himself, and then starts barking at people and turns into the villain. However, when Mom feels like a victim, she's more likely to complain to the kids. Your brother is a sympathetic listener, so he usually starts out the hero. But then, as everyone dumps their problems on him, he, too, turns into a victim.

Now in your notebook or journal, write down some roles your family members take. Then fill in the behaviors that go with each role. You might use a layout like the one below:

Family member: _____

Role: _____

Behavior _____

Now, think of the roles you take on. For instance, you may play the hero by dropping everything to straighten up the house so your dad will stop yelling about how messy it is. Or you may turn into the villain when you lecture your sister to stop whining and assume some responsibility for her life. You may also switch between roles: when you feel guilty, you are a hero moving mountains. When you're angry, you turn into a scolding villain.

Remember, the problem isn't with you or your relatives, per se. The problem is with the roles themselves.

In your notebook or journal, write down some of the roles you take on inside your family. You can use a layout like the one below:

Role: _____

Behavior: _____

BICKERING

Once families start bickering, the roles of victim and villain come into play almost automatically. Just the word "bickering" itself implies whiny aggression, being victim and villain simultaneously. Any family members on hand will be lobbied to take sides. Should you take sides and play hero, bad things are likely to happen.

Family bickering is often an *audience fight*. In an audience fight, the combatants aren't really talking to each other. Instead, they're playing to the crowd, trying to hold up the other side to ridicule and make it look bad. It's part argument and part performance.

For example, Alex was visiting his family when things abruptly went sour. His mother had objected to something his father said, and his father stepped up to defend himself. He accused his wife of being irrational and overly sensitive. She, in turn, told the father that "he'd say anything to get attention." Alex tried cracking a joke to get his parents off the subject, but they weren't to be deflected.

His mother said to Alex that his "dad lived in a dream world." His father said to Alex that his "mother needed to stop being such a nag and learn to be a better wife." Both sides were starting to yell. Losing his temper, Alex yelled at both of them to stop or else he'd leave—right then.

From the father's point of view, the triangle looked like this:

Victim: Dad   **Villain:** Mom

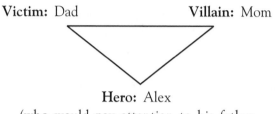

Hero: Alex
(who would pay attention to his father
if only his mother didn't interfere)

From his mother's point of view, the triangle looked like this:

Victim: Mom   **Villain:** Dad

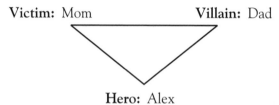

Hero: Alex
(who would pay attention to his mother
if only his father didn't interfere)

Alex tried to be a soothing hero, smoothing over their argument. When that didn't work, he turned into the tough-guy hero, yelling at them both to stop. This worked just about as well as his telling them a joke.

Solution: Remove the Audience

In an audience fight, both sides are performing for the benefit of the audience. Sometimes, if you have been cast as the audience, the most jarring thing you can do is pick up and walk to the exit. In Alex's case he left the room to talk with his sister. After all, his conversation with his parents was over, and he knew their pattern was pretty predictable. At least he could visit with his sister for a while, and rejoin his parents once matters settled down.

By the way, one quick way to end an audience fight during a family gathering is to turn a camcorder on the warring parties. Depending on what works best you might record the two of them dispassionately, as if you were filming a newscast, or enthusiastically as if filming a prize fight. Odds are, they'll settle down quickly.

MELODRAMA

Victims, villains, and heroes are all melodramatic roles. Everything about this syndrome is overblown. There's no room for real people muddling along, the way real people do. People feel obliged to create villains and victims even when there are none.

For instance, Sarah traveled the world as a representative of a nonprofit organization, work she mostly enjoyed except for occasionally being held up at knifepoint. But apart from that she loved her job.

Her grandmother had left Sarah an efficiency condo, in joint ownership with her sister, Violet. Her sister, unfortunately, was a mess. She was currently being evicted from her home, about to lose her job, and had $20,000 in credit-card debt. Violet was certainly no help in taking care of the condo. So, because Sarah traveled so often, one day she decided that it would be best to sell the condo. Sarah thought Violet would be only too happy to agree, considering how much she needed money.

In fact, Violet didn't want to sell. Not stopping there, Violet complained about how badly used she had been regarding the condo and she accused Sarah of ripping her off all the years since their grandmother had died. Working herself into a temper, Violet called their father, whom Sarah rarely saw. Out of the blue she got a furious letter from her dad about the shameful way she was treating her sister.

From Violet's point of view, the pattern looked like this:

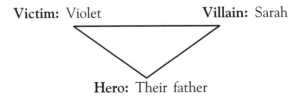

Victim: Violet   **Villain:** Sarah

Hero: Their father

Not knowing what to do, Sarah called her uncle, her dad's brother. While her dad was belligerent, her uncle was the family peacemaker. The uncle helped Sarah to calm down and advised her to send her father a soothing note, and then forget the whole thing, because in a little while her father would forget about it himself.

From Sarah's point of view, the pattern looked like this:

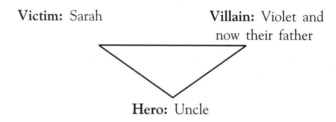

Victim: Sarah   **Villain:** Violet and now their father

Hero: Uncle

The uncle's levelheaded common sense worked. Sarah wrote the letter, but that only quieted her father. This still left the condo and one angry sister.

Sarah could contend with being held up at knifepoint, but she realized she simply could not deal with her sister. What's more, she had to leave the country again and didn't have time to wrangle with her sister, who clearly wasn't listening to her anyway.

Solution: Fight Melodrama with Boredom

The victims and villains syndrome is fueled by melodrama, but it can be dampened with boredom. Remember, problem-solving is sometimes rather boring. Boredom is a vastly underused resource for family fights.

Because Sarah had to leave the country anyway, she delegated the entire mess to her accountant, who happened to be one of the most boring people she knew. The accountant copied all the financial records from the condo and all the tax records, and sent them off to the seething sister. When Violet got his letter, she called him up and raged at him. He sent more paperwork. She raged some more. He sent more files. On occasion he also sent summaries. All of this was as dry as dust.

In the heated contest between Violet's rage and the accountant's boredom, boredom won. Violet agreed to sell. Later, when the accountant spoke to Sarah, he struggled to express his emotions and finally said, "I hate to say this to anyone, but your sister is a loser." Sarah knew there was never an accountant more worthy of his fee.

VOLATILE PROBLEMS

The Toxic Triangle is both treacherous and volatile, but underneath it all, somewhere there's a problem that needs to be solved. Forget the shaming and the melodrama and solve the problem. And what could be more volatile than talking with a teenager about her weight?

Gia's niece, Marci, was seventeen and about seventy pounds overweight. Weight had long been a loaded topic in Gia's family. Half the family was overweight and half was not, depending on which set of genes they had inherited.

Gia's grandmother had been quite thin and a noted beauty, while Gia's mother had been overweight and a frump. Gia grew up listening to her grandmother's merciless attacks on her mother, who buried her misery in eating more ice cream. So, in Gia's life, Grandmother was the villain, her mother was the victim, and Gia was the young, would-be hero, who couldn't possibly solve the problems between these feuding adults.

Two generations later, Gia realized that the family disorder had resurfaced in her niece Marci. Gia wanted to get help for Marci, but she wanted to do it without inflaming the family's pattern. (Along with obesity, members of the family suffered from a host of weight-related diseases, including diabetes, hypertension, and heart disease, so it did need addressing.) Gia didn't care whether Marci was overweight; she cared that her niece be healthy.

Solution: Find the Problem and Solve It

The pattern of victims, villains, and heroes is terrible for solving problems—a point lost on the previous generation in their endless rounds of shame and guilt. A much better plan is to identify the problem and then go solve it.

Rather than risk stirring up the miserable family history, Gia approached this as a forthright medical issue. She knew, for instance, that there would be no shame or implied persecution if her niece had torn her Achilles' tendon. It might be a long, hard recovery and the teen might balk at every turn, but still, the adult thing to do was to create a treatment plan and stick with it because that's what the kid needed.

Gia divorced the problem from any sort of shame or blame. Obesity ran in the family, as did all the other related diseases. Shame was keeping the family from acting in Marci's interest. So, Gia decided to bypass the shame and address the problem.

Her first move was to speak to Marci's parents about finding a new doctor, someone who would treat Marci's weight as a forthright medical condition. Gia, herself, had struggled all her life to control her own weight. During this struggle, she had observed for herself, as well as for many of her relatives, that their appetites didn't function as regulators. Early on, Gia had recognized that she had the same problem: she seldom knew when she was hungry and when she was full. She had had to teach herself all sorts of tricks to tell the difference. Evidently her niece had the same malfunction.

Gia approached the issue as the problem of a nonworking appetite. She talked to Marci about how she had worked this out for herself. And then she persuaded Marci's mom to butt out and leave the rest to professionals, who had none of the loaded family history. As it turned out, the girl had a serious thyroid problem, which probably could have been diagnosed years earlier.

Relatives Played Against Each Other

As the Toxic Triangle gathers speed and whirls around, people wrestle with each other to grab control instead of wrestling with the problems. Faced with a serious problem, family members feel out of control. Then, feeling helpless, they may turn on each other or play family members against each other. This at least provides a feeling of exercising some power, even if it clearly doesn't fix anything.

If the problem is not yours, instead of blaming and overdramatizing you might calmly ask the current victim how he might prefer to solve it. This gives the victim a sense of choice; he can feel in control again. This works especially well when dealing with aging parents or grandparents.

For instance, Gloria's mom had always been a dominant force in the family, and she had no qualms about resorting to threats, bribery, and guilt-tripping other family members in order to maintain her control over them. However, her age was catching up with her and she had started taking falls.

These falls not only threatened Mom, they scared everyone else in the family as well. Mom handled the problem by talking about it in a guilt-inspiring way, while simultaneously denying that it was a real problem and refusing to do anything about it.

Her kids, clearly frightened, badgered her to see a doctor. Mom refused to go, and, instead played the kids against one another (as in, "Honey, could you get me a carton of milk from the store? Your sister doesn't care if I have fresh milk in the house.") Naturally, each kid in turn lost patience and became the new villain, and a new hero had to be called in. The triangle kept spinning. It even became difficult for them not to bully their mother, because she was so resolute in refusing to take care of herself.

Their family triangle looked like this:

Victim: Mom   **Villain:** Whoever tried
                                    to help Mom last

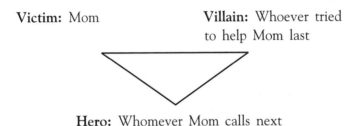

Hero: Whomever Mom calls next

The accusations of heartlessness and not caring may have felt painfully personal, but in fact they were nearly generic. One could plug in any one of the kids at any time and provoke the same accusations from their mother.

Solution: Offer the Victim Choices

You might think this mom had far too much power but, in fact, she felt decidedly powerless. The solution for her family was to disconnect from any guilt or accusations, and give the woman some level-headed choices.

Gloria finally realized that everyone in her family was flooding and her siblings were only making matters worse, so she asked them to back off and let her take a shot at handling things. She knew she needed to stop the whole dynamic of victims and villains. She also had to get her mom to stop playing the victim, if not for her own health's sake, then for the sake of the rest of the family.

Gloria understood that her mom was afraid of losing control, so she thought about how she could put her mother back in the driver's seat. She decided the best plan would be to offer choices.

For instance, if her mom complained about the pain in her hip, Gloria would not step in. Instead, she fought off her flooding, resisted the wave of guilt, and asked her mother which she preferred: Would she rather find a better pain medication, or see a doctor about her hip? If her mom opted for pain medication, Gloria offered more choices: Would she prefer to see a doctor for serious meds, or check what was available over the counter? And so on.

Remember, flooding is contagious, but so is calm. As Gloria asked these questions, her mom would calm down and deal with the issue in a more rational way. Rather than go into accusations or self-pity, her mom would stop and consider what she preferred. Then Gloria would help her get it.

Finally, her mom opted to talk with a surgeon. The doctor took one look at the X-rays and promptly informed Gloria's mom she had to have surgery. Before her mother bridled, Gloria quickly rephrased that as a choice: Would she prefer to have a hip replacement and deal with surgery, or not do surgery and deal with the pain?

Mom opted for surgery, whereupon the surgeon told her that she'd need to spend a few weeks at a rehab facility. Again, her mom was ready to dig in her heels, and again Gloria rephrased the problem as a choice: Mom could either go home with an aide and risk complications, or deal with a rehab center where they dealt with postsurgical patients every day. Mom chose rehab.

This process of choosing went surprisingly well through all the pre-op tasks, until it came time to check out rehabilitation facilities.

Mom had been edgy about extended care centers, but she did pretty well until she actually arrived to inspect the place. As they took the tour, they encountered some long-term nursing home patients drifting around the hallways, looking vulnerable and lost. At that point, Gloria's mom lost her head completely and started yelling at the staff: "I don't have to be here! I've got money. I can pay!" Gloria quickly apologized to the staff, then offered Mom more choices: Would she like to go home or check out the other place? Mom wanted to go home.

Although her mom didn't exactly admit she had panicked, she did own that it had disturbed her to see people her age in a nursing home. Gloria talked her down from flooding, and when Mom was ready, they went to check out another facility.

The second nursing home was primarily for people in postsurgical rehab, so it was quite different. Mom arrived just as some patients were going through their exercises. Rehab isn't easy, of course, but these patients looked strong and determined, not vulnerable or lost. This was something Gloria's mom could live with.

On the drive home, her mother actually asked Gloria questions to evaluate the different rehab facilities: "I like the second one better, but it's a longer drive for you. Would that be okay?" Gloria was amazed to see her mom weighing the pros and cons and discussing matters with her as an adult and peer. This was a first, and it marked a change in their relationship.

Powerlessness will drive people to extremes. The game of victims and villains transforms powerlessness into a club to bludgeon one's nearest and dearest. It may not be very nice, but it sure beats feeling helpless; at least until they've alienated everyone they know.

In the case above, Gloria offered her mother power by rephrasing all of her options as choices, and then helping her mother carry out the choice she made. Had it just been up to Gloria she would have dragged her mother to the surgeon long before, but that wasn't Gloria's call. Ultimately, it was her mother's problem, so it was her mother's place to decide the process.

EXERCISE: OFFERING CHOICES

Offering choices is a particularly good way to deal with victims and solve a given problem. Think of a family member who plays the victim and always gets you hooked into the Toxic Triangle. It could be your mother who won't learn how to drive a car, your father who complains about your mother, or your brother who lives in the basement and complains about them both.

Now, instead of rescuing them like a hero or scolding them like a villain, think of how you might offer them choices. For instance, your mother won't learn how to drive, so you can offer her a choice between: taking lessons from you or from a stranger; signing up for a community ride service; taking a cab; or signing up for delivery service.

Now, below or in your notebook or journal, write down some complaints and choices you might offer, rather than getting embroiled in rescuing your family victim. You might use the following layout as a guide:

Victim complaint: _____

Choice: _____

PERPETUAL MOTION/PERPETUAL ANGER

Victims and villains is such a powerful pattern it can keep going long after the original people who triggered it have died.

For example, Jaylin's dad was a genial old guy who was nice to all the world except his kids. As he lay dying of kidney failure, he refused to see Jaylin who had been something of a hell-raiser in her youth. A few days before he died, he cut her out of his will. The other kids tried to keep this from her, thinking this was no time to fight. She went to see him anyway and he drove her away, telling her that she had been disinherited.

He died. Of all things, she blamed her siblings.

Her siblings were willing to set aside the will and split the money equally, but now Jaylin would have none of it. She didn't want the money and she wanted nothing to do with any of them. Jaylin was now a martyr.

You can sketch it like this:

Victim: Jaylin   **Villain:** Dad and Siblings

Would-Be Heroes:
(siblings who were willing to split
the money to keep the peace)

The stress from her father's death and the ensuing fury put Jaylin into the hospital with renal failure. There, she, in turn, refused to see her family. She was really committed to the victim role. Some distant cousins called to visit, and Jaylin railed against her brothers and sisters and demanded the cousins take sides.

Solution: Decline to Take Sides

This kind of family quarrel is not a football game, where you root for one side or the other. There is no winning this family fight. It's a sad situation, but there's nothing to be gained from taking sides.

Jaylin's cousins simply declined to takes sides. They listened to Jaylin patiently, but said nothing against the other members of the family. First, they didn't know half of what was going on, and second, no good could come of it. It kept the cousins out of the Toxic Triangle and kept things from getting worse. At this point, Jaylin was hurting no one but herself.

Refusal to Negotiate

Playing the game of victims and villains is also a way to avoid negotiating. In the case above, Jaylin wouldn't negotiate with her relations even when they were throwing money at her. The pattern is also a routine way to fend off reality.

For instance, if a family member says to you, "Don't call your father a drunk!" you become the villain, your dad is the victim, and whoever's defending him is the hero. It completely bypasses the issue of whether or not he drinks too much and needs treatment.

To take a different situation, let's say you're concerned about your brother who is living on your parents' couch. Your sister tells you, "That topic is not open for discussion," in a warning tone of voice. If you press the point, she's clearly ready to fight. From your point of view, the roles look like this:

Victim: Parents   **Villain:** Brother

Hero: You, trying to protect your parents

From your sister's point of view, the roles look like this:

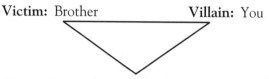

Victim: Brother   **Villain:** You

Hero: Sister who is defending her brother

Solution: Blunt the Drama, Insist on Negotiation

There is a problem that needs to be solved, and it probably can be solved if people sit down and work with each other. However, victims and villains sabotage negotiation. You'll probably have to maneuver the others into negotiating.

When someone puts you in the villain role, the natural impulse is to either counterattack (which makes you even more of a villain) or feel sorry for yourself (which makes you the victim). Instead, try something both surprising and boring: do nothing at first. That is, blunt your reaction.

Naturally, you'll be flooding, so when you feel the surge of adrenaline hit, check your pulse and do what you need to get your flooding under control. Take as much time as you like. Make the relative wait for you. After all, she's the one eager for a fight. If she really wants it, let her wait for it.

When you're ready, calmly say: "What's the problem that needs to be solved?"

If your relative is truly primed for a fight, she'll blast back: "The problem is you!" and she may go on to list your many failings.

Again, show no reaction at all. Do not feed her adrenaline. Keep your hands steady, stay thoughtful, and say, "Okay, but apart from me, what's the problem that needs to be solved?"

At this point your relative might be somewhat exasperated. You haven't sprung at the usual bait. She may repeat herself adding even more faults to the list of what's wrong with you, trying to get you to take up the dance. You can just repeat: "Okay, I got it. You feel I've done many things wrong. But aside from me, what's the problem that needs to be solved?"

By now, you may see your relative struggling to shift gears. Attack hasn't worked. Baiting you hasn't worked. It may be that discussion is all that's left, and that might be hard to face. She might sputter, "Well, well . . ." and maybe her voice will peter out, or maybe she just might help you name the problem to be solved.

Then you can have the discussion that perhaps you should have had a long time ago.

CONTROVERSY

Any major family controversy is likely to trigger a round of victims and villains. Crossing a family taboo will nearly always do it.

Sam's family was Jewish, but he converted to Buddhism after he left college. This remained a touchy subject, and when he was home visiting, he slipped and mentioned a Buddhist tradition. His mother reacted:

Mom: Buddhist—please! Don't mention that word in my presence!

Sam: Mom, it's not a word. It's me. I'm a Buddhist.

Mom: No son of mine would turn his back on his faith.

Mom had a dangerous tone in her voice, and Sam knew if he said another word all hell would break loose.

From Sam's point of view, the situation could be sketched like this:

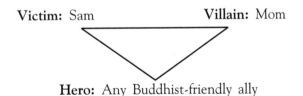

Victim: Sam   **Villain:** Mom

Hero: Any Buddhist-friendly ally

From Mom's point of view, it could be sketched like this:

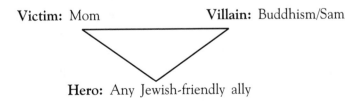

Victim: Mom   **Villain:** Buddhism/Sam

Hero: Any Jewish-friendly ally

Given the family, the identical scenario could be played out over any number of family controversies:

- Dating someone of a different race

- Sexual orientation

- Religious beliefs

- Political beliefs

Now, any family has a set of given boundaries or identities, such as "This family supports the Mayor!" But perhaps some family member feels otherwise. So which is it: Do you support the mayor or do you stop being a member of the family?

The problem is the choice itself. However, since this is a volatile and painful subject, it needs to be handled respectfully. You may choose not to tackle this fight at this time. It might be better to defer this to some family friends or to a support group, if only that they can talk it through more dispassionately.

If you do choose to handle the situation, first control your flooding, then be respectful and maintain civil boundaries:

Sam: Mom, this isn't the time or place, but we need to talk.

Mom: There's nothing to talk about.

Sam: I bet there is. We can talk on the way home tonight.

To handle such a situation, Sam has to allow his mother the space to completely disagree. After all, he was the one to convert to Buddhism, not his mother. She is on a different path than he is, and Sam's had more time to get used to his changes. He probably took months or years to come to his decision, so it isn't realistic to expect his mother to adjust at the drop of a hat.

So, although it is not okay for his mom to embarrass him in public, it is also not okay for him to force her to face things she's not yet ready to face.

People face difficult issues in their own way at their own time. Sometimes the best thing you can do in these circumstances may be to agree not to discuss the subject for now. Trust me, your relative will go on thinking about it while you're not around, and may come to terms with it by a circuitous path. For example, many fundamentalist families have gay and lesbian offspring and cope through the use of unspoken agreements. And though they swear they'll never change, they do change. It happens every day, all around the country. They just don't tell anyone.

Time can do the work that you can't. Be respectful, insist on respect for yourself, but be patient. Even if you're sure you're right, let your relative make his or her changes with dignity.

Note that if the topic is as loaded as your sexual preference or a religious conversion, you should never put a new partner in the middle of the family discussion. That person will become either an instant villain or a victim in someone else's family. That's a thankless role, with no way to win. It's not fair, and it could ruin your relationship.

In dealing with your family, take the worst heat for yourself. Introduce your new partner once things have quieted down.

GUIDELINES

The pattern of victims, villains, and heroes is a form of conflict that is quicksand personified: easy to get into, very hard to get out. Here are some tips for spotting the breakdown and correcting it:

- The three roles—victim, villain, and hero—can switch places with stunning speed. You may start out as the family hero, but you'll become the villain or victim all too quickly.

- Whoever is a hero to one side may well be considered a villain by a different faction.

- These are overblown, melodramatic roles. They don't work for ordinary human beings.

- This pattern is terrible at solving problems. Instead, identify the problem to be solved and go solve it.

- Rather than pitying a victim or feeling guilty, offer him or her choices. Step back and let the person make the decision.

- Playing out the pattern is often a way to avoid reality or negotiating. Blunt the drama and insist on negotiating.

- Any controversy can trigger victims and villains. Be careful about forcing change. Let time do some of the work for you.

EXERCISE: MOVING PAST
VICTIMS AND VILLAINS

Let's say you're fighting with your brother over the tree at your parents' house. He wants to cut it down, because it sheds mountains of leaves and clogs the gutters. You want to save it, because you grew up with that tree.

You think your brother's a villain for wanting to cut down the tree. The tree becomes the victim, and you're the hero who will save it.

Meanwhile, your brother thinks he's the victim, because he's sick of all the yard work. He also considers himself the hero, for shouldering as much as he has done. You're the villain for leaving all the work to him, and then interfering once he's ready to get rid of the tree. It's all pretty easy to sketch.

Now, think of a situation in your own family. Fill in the triangle from your point of view. You can fill it in below or sketch it in your notebook.

Victim: _____   Villain: _____

Hero: _____

Now, think of the same situation from someone else's point of view and sketch it in the triangle. Don't be surprised if the last hero becomes the next villain, or if the villain isn't cast as a victim. Write it below or in your notebook:

Victim: _____   Villain: _____

Hero: _____

Also, don't be surprised if you have no one to name as hero. Heroes get eaten up so quickly in this syndrome that often there's no one left to fill the hero role.

Now, divorce yourself from all these roles, since they don't seem to be working anyway. Think, instead, of the problem to be solved. For instance, in the case of the tree, the problem isn't your stubborn brother. It's that too many leaves are clogging the works.

Now, in your notebook or journal, write down the actual problem underneath all the accusations.

Think of possible solutions for this problem. For instance, in the case of the tree, solutions might include getting screens for the gutters to keep the leaves out, or hiring a local teen to help rake and do yard work.

Think over a range of solutions. Write down at least four in your notebook or journal.

Finally, consider whether the villain in your triangle isn't actually trying to help in a clumsy way. For instance, in the case of the tree, your brother is trying to keep your parents happy. It was just that he feels so overloaded and unappreciated that he has started to think in extremes.

If you now suspect that this "villain" may have been trying to help, think of some kind gesture that might nudge him out of that role. For instance, one man had a sister who was overloaded from looking after their aging parents. Tension was rising between them, so he stepped in to stop the cycle. He brought her flowers, a framed photograph of her and the family, and changed his schedule to give her some relief. She had tears in her eyes as she unwrapped the photo. Someone had finally recognized all the work she'd been doing.

In the case of the tree, you might take your brother out for pizza and talk over ways you could take some of the weight off his shoulders. If nothing else, it may shock him into looking at you with fresh eyes.

Now, in your journal or notebook, write about a kind gesture you might extend to your "adversary."

Chapter Nine

Family Aikido

When relatives exasperate us, we naturally try to change them. We try to get our dad to exercise, or our mom to stop babying us. Soon we learn our efforts haven't worked. People change only when they're ready to change, despite all our arguments and complaints. We can encourage change, lobby for it, and promote it, but we can't force change to happen. Yet, naturally, the more exasperated we become, the more we want to force change, and the more forcing doesn't work.

The Reverend James Bevel worked out an entirely different approach from his experiences as a strategist during the civil rights era. One of his most effective methods was never recorded in his books; instead it was passed along by word of mouth. I had the good fortune to learn it from Phillip Bradley, who worked with Bevel in Chicago.

BEVEL'S PRINCIPLE OF PARTICIPATION

Bevel called his approach the Principle of Participation. The principle holds that rather than trying to change people who will not change, it's better to harness their energies in a positive manner. It's like the martial art Aikido; instead of opposing their power and trying to stop what can't be stopped, you work with their momentum in an unexpected fashion.

Bevel's principle is based on three simple assumptions:

1. We share common interests.

2. We share common outcomes.

3. The other person has a talent for furthering his or her interest as well as your own.

This is to say, you work with your relatives exactly as they are. Instead of fighting their nature, use it.

Perhaps you have an uncle who flaunts his wealth. Excellent! Hit him up for your favorite charity. You may get a check for a good cause, or you may just as quickly discover that it's all an act, and he's up to his ears in debt. One way you get something good from his boasting; the other way you get to quiet the braggart. Either way, you now have a way to deal with your uncle.

How can you make the most of infuriating relatives who will never change their ways? Let's look at some examples.

The Dad Who Wouldn't Talk

My father, like so many men of his generation, didn't talk. By the time he reached his seventies his health began to fail, so I went on a campaign to get to know him better while he was still around.

After a few futile efforts, I realized my dad was profoundly uncomfortable talking, so I thought about where he might feel a little more in his element. Although my dad was not good with people, he was very good with cars, so the next time I came to visit, I asked him if he'd show me how to change my brake pads.

I confess that crawling under a car is not my idea of a great afternoon, but this wasn't about my comfort. It was about his. He thought it was the most normal thing in the world that I should want to change my brake pads myself, and he was happy to show me. I changed into work clothes and we got into it.

Oddly, my dad who didn't talk talked constantly to the car while he worked on it. He muttered to the hex bolts, cursed fondly as he showed me how to wrestle off the wheels, and swore at the engineers who had created tiny, easily lost brake springs. He said more that afternoon than I'd heard him say in months, all addressed to this machine that couldn't talk back. I asked questions, and he explained the mysteries of auto mechanics, along with their evolution and logic.

I learned he thought mechanics were idiots and not to be trusted, and that he had drilled through a finger while working as a mechanist. After some time he started to talk about the factory where he worked, and even talked a little about his life.

It was the first successful conversation I'd ever had with my father, and I learned to build from there. Later on, if we hit another roadblock, I'd drag in something for us to disassemble and put back together.

For my father to have a conversation, he had to do something with his hands. He was most comfortable teaching me things, which was a comfortable role for me as well. Since then it's occurred to me that I too am more comfortable talking when I'm working on something with my hands, so I often do that if someone needs to talk with me. Going back to Bevel's Principle of Participation, here's how it worked with my dad:

1. **Our common interest:** Each other, even though we were strangers in many ways.

2. **Our common outcomes:** He was more interested in cars, while I was more interested in talking. However, I learned to take an interest in cars, and he learned to get used to talking.

3. **His talent:** My dad had a talent for work, not conversation. The best way to reach him was through work.

EXERCISE: REACHING A RELATIVE STRANGER

Many of us have parents or siblings we hardly know at all. The following approach is useful with any relative you wish to get to know better. Here's a step-by-step plan:

1. If you feel frustrated or angry over not being able to reach this person, assume that you're flooding. Since flooding will

leave you trapped in circular thinking and unable to find options, you'll need to deal with your flooding first, before you can be flexible enough to work with this technique.

So first check your symptoms. Is your heart pounding at the thought of talking to this person? Head feeling tight? Has the circular loop of voices started up in your head? Then you're flooding. Get up, walk around, and do your anti-flooding exercises until your head clears.

2.   When you're sure your brain is once again your own, think of the person you wish to get to talk. Where is this person most comfortable? In a fishing boat? On the back porch, with coffee at 7 A.M.? At Wednesday night bingo? In the sauna of a day spa? Cleaning the church sanctuary?

Make a list of those places in your notebook. Remember, these may not be places where you would be comfortable, but places where the other person would be most comfortable.

3.   Now think of activities that this person enjoys. Does she have any hobbies or rewarding commitments? Where is she most herself? Pouring over a stamp collection? Walking with her grandkids? Shopping for bargains? Does he like to hunt for lost golf balls? Or does he like to dig through junkyards for a carburetor for a '63 Mustang?

Write down those activities in your journal. Again, remember, this isn't about what would make you relaxed and happy, but what would make the other person relaxed and happy. Remember that many people are happiest doing something productive, so take this into account.

4.   Now, out of everything you listed, consider which of these places or activities would

(a) be conducive to conversation, and

(b) be something you can stand doing for a few hours.

For instance, you might like to play bingo, but it rarely allows for conversation. Bingo players are usually juggling a lot of cards, and they don't like being interrupted. Still, a relative who enjoys bingo might talk with you on the drive home afterwards, so consider where you might find a window of opportunity.

Write down your best options in your notebook or journal.

Finally, you may go into a situation only to find you don't have a chance to talk after all. For instance, you might join your dad at his bowling league only to discover that he's too busy with his bowling buddies to talk with you. That's okay—you can learn more about your dad by watching him with his pals. Bide your time, and wait for your next window of opportunity. He might be willing to talk on the drive home, or later that night, or even the next day over breakfast when you compare scores.

IMPOSSIBLE RELATIVES

In contrast to relatives who don't talk, you may have relatives who can't stop talking. For example, Carol was once trapped inside her mountain home by two feet of snow, and had to deal with in-laws who drove her crazy. They weren't mean people, just completely self-centered and they never shut up. She couldn't even resort to the time-honored ploy of asking them embarrassing questions about her husband's childhood, since they were so self-centered they didn't even talk about their own kids.

In desperation Carol called her father, who was the most diplomatic person she knew. He gave her two pieces of advice: Try to calm down, and if either of them said anything that was even the tiniest bit interesting to her, ask about it.

She had nothing to lose, and besides, there was always rat poison in the shed. So when they started in again, she waited, and one of them happened to mention the trolley line where he grew up. Trolleys—she could be interested in trolleys! So she asked, and he veered into a monologue about Depression-era trolley cars: how they looked, how they sounded, and how to jump on so the conductor couldn't catch you. After that, they got into greengrocers from the thirties, and what Babe Ruth was like in his prime. They started pulling picture books off the shelves and searching online to see if they could find any photos of the era.

Carol actually enjoyed this. She didn't enjoy it as much as a trip to Vancouver, but some of it was pretty cool and the rat poison stayed in the shed.

1. **Common interests:** Because the in-laws were hideously boring, no common interest was evident at first. But Carol waited until she heard some trace of a common interest. Of course, anything was interesting to the in-laws, as long as they were the ones talking.

2. **Common outcomes:** They had five more days to get through together, and homicide trials aren't fun.

3. **The in-laws have a talent for furthering their self-interest and Carol's:** They could talk. They couldn't stop talking, but they could supply the entertainment. Because they had lived a long time, hearing about one of the eras they had lived through had to be interesting.

EXERCISE: PUTTING A TALKER TO GOOD USE

This technique is useful for interacting with people who are both self-centered and annoying. You won't be able to stop them from being self-centered, but with luck, perhaps you will discover something about them that's entertaining or even enlightening.

1. Again, you'll have to control your flooding first. If you want to strangle these people you will not be able to find something to enjoy. First calm down, then get flexible.

2. Think of the different places they've been and the different eras they've lived through. Which of those are interesting to you? Write them down in your journal or notebook.

3. Now think of historic events they might have witnessed, either in person or on TV; for instance, the walk on the moon, the Kennedy assassination, or the changes in their hometown. Write down the events that might interest you.

4. Next, think of famous individuals or celebrities who were prominent when they were young: Greta Garbo, Groucho Marx, Joe McCarthy, John Kennedy, Billie Holiday, Lucille Ball, Elvis, or Little Richard. Make a list of those you find most interesting.

Now, before you must deal with these people again, do your homework. Scout ahead: where can you find videos or picture books on any of these subjects? For instance, your relatives may love Abbott and Costello or vaudeville comics, but just hearing about their routines isn't as much fun as watching them. Check ahead for a speciality video rental store where you can find some Abbott and Costello and watch the routines together. You can rent an Elvis DVD, or better yet, see if you can catch a local Elvis impersonator. That would have to be a good time.

In a similar fashion, just hearing the history of their hometown may be good, but a photo book on the town's history might be fascinating. You might go out together and find the places mentioned in the book and see how they look now. Your relatives will be interesting in spite of themselves, and you may even find that you like them.

FINDING THE KEY

The idea behind this technique is facing your relations exactly as they are, and then seeing how their quirks—even their flaws—can help solve the conflict. The approach is similar to aikido: instead of resisting them, use their strength to your advantage.

For instance, let's say you have an irritating, deadbeat cousin who never pays back loans. He's been like this for fifteen years. You're not going to change him.

Since he has a clear talent for not repaying loans, put that to good use. Loan him twenty dollars with an absolute deadline for when it's to be paid back. Of course he won't, but then, with luck, he'll avoid you and you won't be troubled by him again.

When you see him at the next gathering, you can pester him for the money, and chase him around the family reunion. You've essentially bought your freedom for twenty dollars. It's a deal worth considering.

Now, the first two steps (looking for common interests and common outcomes) will focus your attention. They provide a way to locate an angle that will appeal to both of you. In the example above, your common interest is twenty dollars. The common outcome is that you both are eager for your cousin to pocket the money.

The crucial step—and the trickiest—is to find the hidden talent that will serve both of you. In this case it's your cousin's unwillingness to pay back what he borrows. But the real trick is to completely change your mind-set. Instead of being annoyed, or indignant, or frustrated by this intractable trait, look for ways it might serve you.

After fifteen years, you already know how your cousin will behave. You now have to discover how to harness his behavior for good.

Let Go of the Infuriating

In order to find that key talent that will further both your relative's interests and your own, you need to set aside your anger. A solution might pop out at you if you look at the situation with fresh eyes.

A fresh approach is essential. When we're angry at relatives, we're usually angry in an old, exceedingly stale fashion. If we check our thoughts, we'll likely find that we've been angry in the same way, for the same reasons, for years. Anger is oddly captivating. We can replay the same anger endlessly and never get bored or tired of it.

If your old anger hasn't delivered a solution yet, it's probably not going to in the future. It's a tool that's not working, so you may as well put it aside. Try something else. You can always go back to the old anger later, when you have time to kill. Meanwhile, try something new. It doesn't have to be brilliant; just break the pattern to amuse yourself. Then keep your eyes open and see if anything interesting transpires.

■ Marie's Story

Marie is a gracious and tactful individual, which is good because she'd married into a family that would drive most people crazy. She had looked after her partner's mom through a lengthy illness, which entailed moving most of the mom's belongings into their house so Mom could be surrounded by familiar things. After she died, Marie wanted her house back, but her partner's brothers and sisters put off dealing with the furniture and knickknacks. Naturally, there was a period of time when they couldn't face sorting through things, but time dragged on and they still did nothing. After a while all the clutter was driving Marie crazy.

One day Marie decided that if all this stuff was going to be around, at least she might try getting some use out of it. So she took a vase, polished it and put it in the living room. Then, when one of her sisters-in-law visited, the in-law saw the vase, said, "That was my mother's," and took it.

This was infuriating but Marie is resourceful, and instead of getting angry, she soon realized this was a way to get her mother-in-law's things out of her house. From then on, whenever one of her in-laws came over, she would polish something she wanted removed and put it on display. Each time the relative would say, "That was Mom's" and take it.

Let's look at this according to Bevel's Principle of Participation:

1. **Common interest:** All their mother's stuff.

2. **Common outcomes:** Getting the mother's stuff out of Marie's house.

3. **The talent that served both of them:** The in-laws were quick to take offense at anyone else enjoying their mom's stuff. So Marie had only to make a show of enjoying it to have her relatives cart it away.

EXERCISE: PUTTING ASIDE ANGER

1. Picture the person who usually gets you angry. No doubt you'll be flooding, so be sure to do flood control before you start.

2. With your flooding under control, consider the usual ways you get angry with this person. For instance, you may say very little in a phone call, then vent after you've put down the phone. Or you may offer advice, have your advice rejected, then fume when your advice would have worked.

    List your usual behavior when you get angry with this person in your notebook or journal.

3. Now, assume that your actions haven't yet produced the results you want. For instance, your offers of advice haven't yet gained you acknowledgment from your family or

gratitude for your helpfulness. In fact, for all you know, your offers might be annoying people. Certainly they haven't gained you any points.

This time, picture something you can do that's totally different from your usual pattern. For instance, when tempted to offer advice you might take the dog out for a walk instead. Or you might go out to the backyard and strike up a conversation with the neighbors about their tomatoes.

It really doesn't matter what you do, as long as it's a complete departure from your usual pattern. Give yourself extra points if you can think of something you would enjoy anyway.

Now, in your notebook, write down three different things you might do that are entirely different from your usual pattern.

4.   The next time you see your family and are tempted to get angry and fall into old ways, take out your list and try something else. Bear in mind that you have no idea how they might react to your change in plans. Watch for anything unexpected. For instance, in Marie's case, she was surprised to see her in-laws cart stuff away once she started using it.

Be alert for openings. For instance, if you stop offering advice and instead admire the neighbors' tomato plants, you may walk away with an armful of tomatoes and hear some interesting hometown gossip.

After you try this, make note of any new development in your journal.

UNSOLICITED ADVICE

We often offer advice in the hope of being helpful, or perhaps to be acknowledged for being intelligent and competent. This often backfires. It's easy to see why if you consider how you feel when someone offers you unsolicited advice.

Most families are generous with unwanted advice. You may be dealing with a new baby, an aging parent, or a fractious teenager—

someone, somewhere will tell you what to do. Once, while wheeling my mother out of the hospital I had a twelve-year-old stranger stop to offer me minute instructions on how to push a wheelchair.

At the time, I was merely exhausted and annoyed. Had I been alert I might have wondered how a twelve-year-old knew so much about wheelchairs, and asked the kid about that.

The problem with unsolicited advice is that you are probably already overloaded and running on your last nerve. The last thing you need is someone lecturing you.

When someone gives you advice on a better way to handle things, rather than snap at that person, promptly suggest that he do it. If he says, "You should really get your mother to stop smoking," suggest that he sit right down and talk with her about it. You can listen in. If it works, you have just learned a good approach. If not, you just won some peace from this person.

The avenues for unwanted advice are endless. For instance, let's say you're dealing with an ailing parent. Someone says to you: "You should really talk to these doctors and get a straight answer out of them."

Your response: "You know, I've got the phone number right here. Why don't you give them a call? Maybe you can get the information."

If that person's approach works, great! If not, it teaches her to appreciate what you've been going through and to stop nagging you about it.

There are so many things in life that "should" happen. It "should" be easy to get a clear answer from Social Security, or a straight answer from your father about his finances, or a forthright prognosis from a doctor. However, instead of getting a straight answer, you plunge into a rabbit warren of bureaucrats, waiting on hold, and doublespeak. If someone else thinks she can cut the Gordian knot, excellent! Offer to hold her coat while she has at it. Don't forget to bring something to read.

In fact, feel free to hand out assignments. If you're dealing with a major family crisis it may be the only way you're likely to get through things.

The formula here is almost generic:

1.   **Common interest:** Whatever's going wrong.

2.   **Common outcomes:** Anything that would fix things.

3. **Hidden talent:** If that person has a way to solve the problem, there's no time like the present. Recruit him immediately.

EXERCISE: HARNESSING WELL-WISHERS

Now you try it.

1. In your journal or notebook, list the unwanted advice you get from your family. Use as many pages as you need. Make particular note of maddeningly difficult things like getting your schizophrenic brother to take his medicine, or improving your stock portfolio. If the task is easy, don't bother. Harness your relatives for the hard jobs.

   Write down your list in your notebook.

2. Now, think of ways you might immediately recruit some relatives to actually do the work and not just talk about it. For instance, if they say you really ought to talk to your brother about his meds, have them sit down and do exactly that. You can watch attentively.

   Now, write down how you could hand over the work that needs to be done.

ANNOYANCE AS A BARGAINING CHIP

Just as your relatives and siblings have ways to irritate you, you may also have ways that irritate them. This means you have something to trade.

To a particularly exasperating sister you might say, "Darla, I will make you an offer. I would really like it if you never mention my ex-husband again. I know you were crazy about Brian and thought he was the best thing that ever happened to me, but I just don't want to hear about it anymore. So, there must be something I do that drives you crazy. I will trade you one monumentally annoying habit of mine in exchange for you not bringing up Brian again."

Now, your sister may drive a hard bargain. She may demand that you drop your superior attitude about your Stairmaster or never again bug her about her smoking. You may face some tough negotiating, but this may bring her around. And if she slips and mentions that great promotion Brian just got, you can always lean over and say, "I'm up to forty-five minutes on the Stairmaster. Four times a week." If your sister knows what's good for her, she'll shut up.

1. **Common interest:** Your mutual ability to annoy each other.

2. **Common outcomes:** You both would like to coexist, hopefully in an easier manner.

3. **Hidden talent:** You both have a special talent for irritating each other, and can both turn it off if you apply yourselves.

EXERCISE: BARGAINING WITH ANNOYANCE

1. Take out your notebook or journal and list the ways a specific member of your family annoys you.

2. Now, consider some ways that you already might be annoying the same relative. List those ways in your notebook.

3. Now check off which of your annoying habits you would be willing to give up in an exchange.

Here are a few things to keep in mind when you present your bargain.

- You won't really know what it is that your relative will wish to trade for. Keep an open mind.

- Be prepared to remind the relative if he slips. After all, he's probably never swapped anything like this before.

- Keep your sense of humor. You may as well be good-natured about this.

HOSPITALS

Family members can be particularly exasperating in hospitals, to no small degree because you're worried and feel somehow responsible. Sick people can be remarkably uncooperative, even when they're seriously ill and ought to know better.

The problem is in the nature of hospitals themselves. People become reduced to a disease and stripped of their identities. They become "The kidney stone" rather than "Mr. Smith." Much of the rebellion and uncooperativeness they exhibit is their way of asserting themselves in a situation where they feel out of control.

For instance, one young woman would put on her clothes every morning and go across the street to have breakfast at a diner and smoke a cigarette. She was in for pneumonia.

Afterwards, she would walk back upstairs to her hospital room, change back into her gown, and make excuses about not eating what was on her tray.

It wasn't that she was a hopeless addict. It was that this was the only way she had of feeling like herself for an hour and a half every morning, before she had to go back and submit to doctors again.

I was once in the hospital for a long stay and ended up losing my spleen, which meant major surgery. A few days after the operation there were fireworks in the neighborhood, so my friends wheeled me out of my room, outrunning the nurses, and took me to a skyway where we watched the show.

I laughed myself silly, and laughing really hurt. I didn't care. For the first time in weeks I felt like a human being.

When you have a relative defying the doctors, the instinct is to pressure him into doing as he's told. This only means your family member now will need to defy you as well as the doctors. But there is another way.

Give the patient some other way he can assert his individuality. For instance, he might miss his dog very much. It would be too unwise to try to smuggle the dog into the hospital, but you could make a tape recording of the dog barking and play the tape to your relative.

You could include a mock translation. Perhaps you could have a debate about your translation as to what the different barks mean. You could also snap pictures of the dog and provide a narration. And you could do the same for a baby, a grandchild, or the patient's garden.

You may be concerned that your relative isn't worried enough about himself or invested enough in getting better. It may be he needs a break from worrying about himself. Instead he may need to feel normal again, with the normal things that make up life. Bring life in with you to the hospital, give it to him, and give him a chance to laugh about it.

The more you give patients a chance to reassert themselves, the more likely it is they will be able to tolerate the strangers in white uniforms.

You can see how this breaks down according to Bevel:

1. **Common interest:** The patient's well-being.

2. **Common outcomes:** Getting the patient well and out of the hospital as soon as possible.

3. **Hidden talent:** The patient's need to assert him- or herself can cause a lot of problems if it isn't redirected. Be imaginative, then supply alternatives.

WORK FROM STRENGTH

If someone you love is ill or has had a serious injury, she may not think as well as she used to. That's frightening. Even so, you have to contain your fear and figure out how to deal with her in the here and now.

As long as she's conscious, there will still be some area where she is competent. Find it and build on it.

For instance, Phil's father came out of surgery and suddenly couldn't remember simple things. Brain problems can be a side effect of too much time hooked up to a heart and lung machine, and Phil wasn't warned beforehand. Sometimes the effects wear off and sometimes not. His father was a dynamic man, and it was hard for Phil to see him this way.

Meanwhile, Phil had watched all sorts of people telling his dad what to do and offering advice. He knew how irritating this was for himself, and he thought it must be even more galling for someone his father's age. So Phil started a policy of asking his father for advice. He didn't expect much, but he thought it might make his father feel more like himself.

As it happened, Phil cut his hand while staying at his father's home, and he asked his dad about first aid in the house. His father reeled off the exact medications to be found in each cabinet, which shelves they were on, and the pros and cons of each medication. Phil was startled, to say the least. Evidently his father's long-term memory was intact, even though his short-term memory was impaired.

Phil kept it up. He asked his father's advice on back-lighting his laptop, and his dad directed him to four different lamps, described their advantages, and gave him the location of a lighting shop where Phil might find replacement bulbs.

After a while, his father's short-term memory began to come back. He started telling family stories without repeating himself and he even told some new ones. With incentives, his brain had started to rewire itself, with other cells taking over for the damaged ones. His personality came back. Curiously, he would still lapse and play stupid when someone told him what to do, but the rest of the time he was a pleasure to be around.

Let's look at this according to Bevel's Principle of Participation:

1. **Common interest:** Phil's father.

2. **Common outcomes:** Getting Phil's dad thinking and functioning again.

3. **Hidden talent:** They were both surprised to find that part of his father's brain was nearly fully functional. By playing to his dad's strengths, instead of treating him like an invalid, Phil got him back and reengaged.

BEING NEEDED

Relatives can also get tired of being invalids, especially if they've spent their lives being needed. Rather than babying them, you might try finding ways they can contribute.

Consider Donna, who had always been an active and highly respected woman in her community, until bad health forced her to move in with her daughter in a different part of the country. She disliked the loss of her independence, having to do exercises, and taking orders. Her health continued to deteriorate, which then forced her into a nursing home.

Some people might get depressed, but Donna got angry. Then things got worse. She lost one leg, than another, which meant no way out of the nursing home.

This is the point where many people give up and die, but Donna unexpectedly stabilized, then blossomed. The change was so striking I interviewed her at the nursing home to see what had happened to change her spirits so.

Evidently, two things had changed. First, she'd settled into her own room at the long-term care facility, which gave her a space to claim as her own. Second, she realized how hard everyone worked at the home, and she saw that the only way the place could function was if everyone cooperated. In short, something important was needed from her.

In the interview, Donna didn't talk about herself as a woman with health problems. She talked about herself as a soldier on a tough assignment. She understood the staff were counting on her to work with them, and she was determined to pull her own weight. She wasn't going to let them down.

1. **Common interest:** The long-term care facility.

2. **Common outcomes:** Keeping the place functioning.

3. **Hidden talent:** Donna didn't need to be babied. She needed a tough assignment that would demand all her strength and resourcefulness.

SECRET BLESSINGS

Sometimes we get annoyed over things that are really advantages. For instance, you may have a relative who leaves irritable messages on your answering machine. It may irk you that she won't deal with you in a more straightforward manner. But is it really so bad that she yells at your machine, rather than at you?

People who chew out machines are often conflict-avoidant. They may not have the nerve to say these things to you directly. They may not sound afraid as they spit fire into your digital recorder, but if they were all that confident, they'd take their satisfaction chewing you out in person, rather than barking at a machine that can't bark back.

Listen to the message once to check for any crucial information, such as, "I'm tired of cat-sitting, come get your stupid animal." In that case, you have a problem to solve and you'd best go deal with it.

Resist the urge to play the rant again. That will only get you worked up and give that relative everything she wants. Instead, erase the message. When you talk with her next, mention how unreliable your answering machine is and how you don't get half of your messages. If she still has something to get off her chest, she can bring it up then. She'll probably be tamer the second time around.

If you're conflict-avoidant as well, you also have the option of dealing with her only by answering machine. The machine becomes your buffer zone, and your life becomes more peaceful.

THEY DEMAND, YOU FLEE

Perhaps the worst of all the parental pressures is when nothing you do is ever enough.

For instance, your mom loves you and misses you, so she nags you. Being nagged, you stay away. So, naturally, you feel guilty; but when you come in closer, she's upset because of having missed you, so she nags you. So you stay away—and feel guilty.

You wouldn't know it, but you're both actually trying to coexist, you're just doing it in such a way that is driving you apart. There is actually a name for this: *complementary schismogenesis*. "Complementary" means both sides are working together. "Schismo" (as in schism) means split or divided. Finally, "genesis" means to create. So "complementary schismogenesis" means that both sides are working together to create a division.

The term was coined by the anthropologist Gregory Bateson (1936), but it doesn't just refer to anthropology. The same breakdowns happen within families as well.

Families can be masters of the complementary schismogenesis. Your dad doesn't like what you're doing, so he criticizes you. Being criticized, you defy him. Since you refused to listen and are defying him, he criticizes you more. Under the barrage of criticism, you shut down completely and refuse to even discuss the subject. Both sides are trying to fix something, but they end up setting each other off and making the situation worse.

The solution, strangely, is to abruptly hit reverse. Do the exact opposite of whatever you've been doing. Instead of defying your father, call him up and ask for his advice on an inoffensive topic. Instead of running away, step closer. If it's a schismogenesis, you'll get a wave of sudden relief.

For example, Luis was bright, hardworking, and lived at home. He had a demanding job and took night classes in addition to his full-time work. His mother complained that she never saw him anymore, that he was becoming a stranger. He tried to explain to her that he was already under a great deal of pressure.

Rather than listen to him, his mother nagged him. The more she nagged, the more he avoided her. They loved each other but they were making each other crazy.

Once Luis realized there was a schismogenesis going on, he abruptly hit reverse. Instead of burying himself in homework, he took his mother to breakfast. All his life she had made breakfast for the family, so he took her someplace nice, just the two of them.

Once there, they talked, and he told her all he could about his life. He also told her how special she was and how much he loved her, and how completely overloaded he was at that particular time. For the first time, she seemed to hear him.

His mother stopped nagging him, and Luis stopped running away from her. And, hopefully, before the breakdown got out of hand again, he took her out to breakfast again to talk and remind her she was special.

Now you may think that this kind of action is unnecessary. Of course she's special. She's your mom; how many moms do you have? Who else could make you feel so guilty? But because you know she's special doesn't mean she knows it, and running away isn't exactly a signal that she's a central person in your life.

SUPPLY AND DEMAND

The hard-to-satisfy parent is a particularly difficult problem. It's all too easy to slide into the past and get bogged down in the family quicksand rather than acting like the modern, resourceful adult that you are.

One way to escape old patterns is to look at the situation in terms of supply and demand. Look around for something that your relative always wanted and asked for, but never got. This can become your peace offering or bargaining point. Note that it may not be a physical object.

For instance, perhaps your mother always said what she wanted in life was for you to get along with your brother. Okay. As a gesture to her, for one day you can make it a point to be nice to your brother.

In a similar vein, she may have always done things for you that no one ever did for her. For instance, if she's always made hot chocolate for you on cold days, then the next time it's cold, you make hot chocolate for her.

If you come from a family where no one says, "I love you," say, "I love you Mom." If you come from a family where no one makes time, make time.

If no one in your family ever says, "Mom, you were right," then make up a list of all the times she was right, and present it to her. Write it down, or even sketch it if you're not good with words. You can even clip pictures from a magazine if you like, but give her something she can hold in her hands and look at on the bad days.

If your mother already has all these things, then just give her a picture of the two of you together, and tell her everything you can remember about the day that photo was taken, and how you remember her. These are all things she hasn't had that are bound to make an impression.

Bragging Rights

As you strategize ways to build a bridge to a difficult parent, remember the value of bragging rights. For instance, when Luis took his mother out to breakfast, he gave her something unusual to talk about with her circle of friends. She not only got the attention she wanted, she also got a story to tell.

Parents are human. They like to show off for their friends sometimes. If you can produce a framed picture of the two of you together—with the story of the day the picture was taken, fifteen years ago, you will have given your parent something to show their buddies. None of their friends will have this. The sheer scarcity of the gift will make it something to remember.

LOCKED IN PLACE

Finally, you may be locked into old patterns with family members where you both know what you're doing and both hate it. Even so, neither of you can manage to stop. You may have done a world of therapy, read every self-help book in creation, and have profound insights into precisely what you're doing. You both have done this, and in spite of all your efforts, somehow you still exasperate each other. You've had no success in breaking these patterns. What then?

If you simply can't get the best of these patterns, instead of fighting them, run with them. Let's say you designate one day a week when your mother can oppress you and you can defy her. Make it Tuesday.

You can then act out for all you're worth on Tuesday. The rest of the week, the two of you can relax and act like normal people. It becomes a joke. You might learn some things.

"Hey, Mom, it sounds like we're having a Tuesday. Could we flip the calendar?"

Carla Thomas, a veteran teacher who's terrific with kids, uses a variation of this approach with fractious children. Let's say you're tending your brother's four-year-old who likes to kick. Say, "Okay, here's the chair to kick. Kick this chair until I tell you to stop." Then keep the kid at it until he or she is thoroughly sick of kicking.

With little kids you can do this with any bad habit. "You're spitting? All right, here's the spitting corner. You stand right here and spit until I say you can stop."

You have them keep it up until it isn't fun anymore. In fact, instead of kicking and spitting being acts of defiance, kicking and spitting becomes a way of following orders. Any kid is going to get sick of that fast.

GUIDELINES

This chapter is based on the Rev. James Bevel's Principle of Participation, which consists of three assumptions:

1. We share common interests.

2. We share outcomes.

3. The other person has a talent for furthering his or her own interest, and my own.

The test, therefore, is how to find that talent and harness it. To accomplish this you will need to:

- Keep your flooding under control.

- Forget about being angry for a while. If it's important, you can always go back to being angry later.

- Look for blessings in disguise. Your relative's strongest and most irritating traits can be harnessed to produce something positive and good.

- Beware the complementary schismogenesis, where you continue to fuel the breakdown even as you're trying to fix the situation.

- Make use of supply and demand. Anything in short supply (kind words, affection) may have a particularly compelling power.

- Keep in mind any parent's secret desire for bragging rights.

- If you and your relative simply can't change, then at least limit your acting-out to one day a week. The rest of the time you can relax.

Family bonds are beyond understanding. Our relatives may be exasperating and infuriating down to their DNA. Still we love them. There's no explaining it. We just have to deal, and be grateful knowing that however much we infuriate them, they love us too, in their way.

Hopefully, we can find ways to survive all this love. Perhaps the key is compassion. Compassion has always been less painful than love, and easier to withstand. Compassion is rarer in families, and asks a bit more of us. But compassion, good sense, and just a little bit of wiliness can make the trek home a more livable experience.

References

Bateson, Gregory. 1936. *Naven*. Cambridge, England: Cambridge University Press.

Bradshaw, John. 1995. *Family Secrets: What You Don't Know Can Hurt You*. New York: Bantam Books.

Dickinson, Amy. 2005. Drunken dad has his work cut out for him. *Chicago Tribune*, May 16, Chicagoland final, CN edition, section 5, p. 2.

Gottman, John, and Nan Silver. 1995. *Why Marriages Succeed or Fail: What You Can Learn from Breakthrough Research to Make Your Marriage Last*. New York: Simon & Schuster.

Hoffman, Virginia. 2005. Medea's Conflict Continuum. (lecture n.d.) Loyola University, Chicago, IL.

Kennedy, Lt. John. 1993. Hostage Negotiation (lecture, n.d.) Center for Conflict Resolution, Chicago, IL.

Medea, Andra. 2004. *Conflict Unraveled: Fixing Problems at Work and in Families*. Chicago: PivotPoint Press.

Moss, Barbara Robinette. 2004. *Fierce*. New York: Scribners.

Satir, Virginia. 1988. *The New Peoplemaking*. New York: Science and Behavior Books.

Scheflen, Albert E., with Alice Scheflen. 1972. *Body Language and the Social Order: Communication as Behavioral Control*. Englewood Cliffs, NJ: Prentice Hall.

Seligman, Martin E. P. 1992. *Helplessness: On Depression, Development, and Death*. New York: W. H. Freeman.

Tannen, Deborah. 1984. *That's Not What I Meant!* New York: William Morrow.

Tannen, Deborah. 1989. *You Just Don't Understand: Women and Men in Conversation*. New York: William Morrow.

Van Buren, Abigail. 2005. Dear Abby. *Chicago Tribune*, July 11, section 5, p. 8.

OTHER NEW HARBINGER TITLES

How to Stop Backing Down and Start Talking Back
A feisty and fiery guide to telling it like it is without taking any guff
Item 4178, $13.95

Self-Esteem, Third Edition
A user's guide to a good, valuable, and important person—you!
Item 1985, $15.95

The Daughter-in-Law's Survival Guide
Don't wait for his mother to start understanding you! These techniques can lead to interfamily peace fast
Item 2817, $12.95

Talk to Me
This collection of tips for the small-talk challenged will get you glib in no time
Item 3317, $12.95

Letting Go of Anger, Second Edition
Identify the eleven most common anger styles and make them work for you
Item 4488, $15.95

Children of the Self-Absorbed
Techniques for coping with the legacy of narcissistic parents
Item 2310, $14.95

The Messages Workbook
Say what you mean every time with this communication classic
Item 3716, $19.95

Watercooler Wisdom
Smart ways to manage conflict, pressure, and change in the workplace
Item 4364, $14.95

available at bookstores nationwide

To order, call toll free, **1-800-748-6873,** or visit our online bookstore at **www.newharbinger.com**. Have your Visa or Mastercard number ready.

Prices subject to change without notice.

HILLSBORO PUBLIC LIBRARIES
Hillsboro, OR
Member of Washington County
COOPERATIVE LIBRARY SERVICES